Already Missional

Already Missional
Congregations as Community Partners

Bradley T. Morrison

Foreword by
Rob Dalgleish

RESOURCE *Publications* • Eugene, Oregon

ALREADY MISSIONAL
Congregations as Community Partners

Copyright © 2016 Bradley T. Morrison. All rights reserved. Except for brief quotations in critical publications or reviews, no part of this book may be reproduced in any manner without prior written permission from the publisher. Write: Permissions. Wipf and Stock Publishers, 199 W. 8th Ave., Suite 3, Eugene, OR 97401.

Resource Publications
An Imprint of Wipf and Stock Publishers
199 W. 8th Ave., Suite 3
Eugene, OR 97401

www.wipfandstock.com

PAPERBACK ISBN: 978-1-4982-7912-3
HARDCOVER ISBN: 978-1-4982-7914-7

Manufactured in the U.S.A.   01/11/2016

New Revised Standard Version Bible, copyright 1989, Division of Christian Education of the National Council of the Churches of Christ in the United States of America. Used by permission. All rights reserved.

Chapter 1: Already Missional adapted from Morrison, Bradley T. "Already-Mission: Expanding Congregational Mission." *Missiology: An International Review.* 42 (2014) 271-83.

Contents

Foreword by Rob Dalgleish | vii
Acknowledgments | ix

Introduction | 1

Part One: Missional Opportunity | 13
Chapter 1: Already-Missional | 15

Part Two: Missional Vision | 31
Chapter 2: Missional Strategy | 33
Chapter 3: Missional Focus | 42

Part Three: Missional Structure | 53
Chapter 4: Missional Ministries | 55
Chapter 5: Missional Support | 68

Part Four: Missional Culture | 77
Chapter 6: Missional People | 79
Chapter 7: Missional Partnerships | 88

CONTENTS

Part Five: Missional Assets | 97

Chapter 8: Missional Property | 99
Chapter 9: Missional Finances | 108

Conclusion | 119

Bibliography | 121

Foreword

I LIKE TO SAY that God is up to something big in our generation! The problem is the church so rarely acts as though we believe it. More and more, it's not a lack of awareness about the need for change that's at stake. It's an apparent lack of capacity to move towards change in any coherent way.

What if we were actually able to orient the passions and gifts, needs and yearnings of all our people towards a singular purpose, to live out God's dream for the world starting with their church in their local community? What might become possible?

For me, *Already Missional* rises out of the landscape of God's great work of love in a transitioning world. It offers a practical tool to not only chart, but pursue a course of deep meaning and vital mission. It offers a way to unleash people's passion and gifts and then, in love, *do something* about it together. The processes suggested, if well facilitated, can hold generative space for the kind of conversations that really matter, and through which all change comes about.

When I read Brad's book I immediately fell in love with the premise, already-missional. In my work with Edge in the United Church, I have too often seen churches make the fatal error of ignoring the deep yearning and vocation of individuals when thinking about congregational mission. This diffuses energy, exhausts

FOREWORD

people and paralyzes mission. I get really excited about the potential of this book for engaging the already-mission treasure of passion, purpose and action that is a natural part of people's everyday lives. Like all brilliant insights it is obvious once seen and also effective in shifting the imagination in the work of turning to missional preparedness.

This book gives energy rather than using it up. Brad skillfully weaves a tapestry of historical and theoretical grounding, transformative insight, effective educational process, and solid organizational practice. The tool is adaptive by nature and therefore well suited to the emerging cultural context. It provides practical ways to see and attend to how mission is moving forward (or not) and to adapt when actions or outcomes don't match intention or hopes. Even more, it comes out of the experience of an effective congregational leader.

Edge consultants are working in one form or another with hundreds of congregations across the church. There are a very few things I could see being worthwhile to encourage engaging in almost all of them. Brad's book would be one of them.

Brad, thanks for doing it!

Rev. Rob Dalgleish
Executive Director
Edge: A Network for Ministry Development

Acknowledgments

THIS BOOK EVOLVED FROM a convergence of partnerships. Thank you to Grace United Church in Sarnia, Canada for supporting a sabbatical and subsequent study leaves that made it possible to ponder and write iterations of this resource. Thank you for the many already-missional conversations with parishioners and people in the community.

Thank you to Huron University College in London, Canada and the students in my congregational development and leadership course. The refining of this book's ideas and testing of the interview questions in multiple congregations relied on student commitment to field-based learning.

Thank you to Rob Dalgleish, director of the Edge Network for encouraging the book. Thank you to the Edge Network consultants for using earlier iterations of this resource with congregations.

My biggest thank you goes to Sarah and our children—partners in and center of my already-mission.

Introduction

IN AN ACTIVE, NEIGHBORHOOD congregation, a room full of young parents gather for a baptismal preparation meeting with the minister. Mostly first-time parents, the participants have newborns and toddlers in arms. Some parents look tired, and others seem energized to have an evening out with other parents. The minister engages the group in a conversation about their sense of purpose as parents. Parents are asked a simple question: How can this congregation support you with your parenting mission? Rather than discussing how parents can participate in Sunday school and family programs, the minister keeps the conversation focused on the parenting mission that participants have in common. The minister offers the congregation as a partner in that parenting mission.

A newcomer to the congregation shares with the minister how he travels to his native Philippines periodically to rescue young girls trapped in the nation's sex trade industry. The minister recognizes God already at work in this newcomer's personal mission. The newcomer is given time during Sunday morning announcements to describe his activity to the congregation, which leads to financial support. A few months later, the newcomer-turned-parishioner is selected as a finalist in a national funding competition, which includes a film crew documenting a trip to

INTRODUCTION

the Philippines for national broadcast.[1] The parishioner sees the congregation as a partner in his rescue mission.

A group of parishioners support a local agency involved in international development and aid. Many of these congregational members have participated in poverty awareness trips and serve the organization as leaders and volunteers. The devastating 2012 earthquake in Haiti, where the agency operates and supports a number of rural development agencies and schools, brings parishioners together to explore how they can support their agency's mission on short notice. An ecumenical, interfaith worship service and fundraiser is organized quickly, and extra-congregational networks of volunteers are accessed for support.[2] A second event is held the following year with an expanded multicultural festival,[3] leading to increased participation by other parishioners with the international aid agency. The aid agency sees the congregation, through its parishioners, as a partner in their international development work.

In the wake of a series of student suicides in the community, the congregation organizes a screening at the local movie theatre of a documentary on bullying. The event includes a panel discussion with local experts and the community.[4] The congregation draws on parishioner connections to partner with over a dozen local agencies to sponsor the event. Over five hundred people from the community participate. After the event, parishioners continue to engage local agencies and government on the issue. Because the congregation valued and nurtured parishioner relationships with established community agencies, parishioners connected congregational assets with community assets to impact the community.

These are stories about a missional congregation. Missional, put simply, means being God's good news in your community and the world. Missional congregations do more than talk about God's good news, they *are* good news by meeting actual needs in their

1. Sandborn, "Top 50."
2. Persichetti, "Diverse Faiths."
3. Rayjon, "Gathering of Hope."
4. Wright, "Organizers Hope the Movie *Bully* Sparks Discussion."

INTRODUCTION

community. Healthy congregations are missional. Your congregation is a vital part of God's mission in the world. Every community is different, so every congregation is called to be good news in a unique way. Missional-minded congregations begin with an awareness that parishioners are already on mission at home and in the community. Missional congregations figure out how to value, nurture, and partner with these already-missions.

This book is written for congregational leaders, and the book's goal is to help your congregation to improve its missional readiness. The questions that guide each chapter were developed and tested in a variety of congregations from multiple denominations.[5] Each chapter draws on principles from the missional church movement,[6] which understands that *how* we are the church (ecclesiology) depends on *why* we are the church (missiology).

This introductory chapter is written with pastoral leaders and congregational consultants in mind, focusing on missiological themes and change strategies guiding the rest of the book. Most readers may want to skip to the summary section at the conclusion of this introductory chapter. From there, the book will discuss how you can nurture missional thinking and community partnerships in your congregation.

Missional Church

The missional church movement reminds us that the church is not an end unto itself.[7] Rather, the church exists to serve God's mission.

---

5. The assessment questions were developed over a five-year period, and these iterations were tested by students in my congregational development course at Huron University College in London, Canada. Congregations included Anglican, United Church, Presbyterian, Christian Reformed, Baptist, Disciples of Christ, and community/non-denominational.

6. The missional church movement traces its roots back to the influence of Lesslie Newbigin and the Gospel and Our Culture Network. The term was popularized with the publication of Guder, *Missional Church*.

7. An inwardly focused church is ecclesiocentric. The ecclesia (Greek *ekklesia* for assembly or congregation) becomes self-centered rather than mission-focused. The missional church movement understands the *ekklesia* or

INTRODUCTION

When a congregation is mistakenly focused inwardly, the congregation's survival becomes the mission. A missional congregation, however, is shaped and formed by an understanding of God's vision for the world. Worship, programs, budgets, and people are stewarded for participation in God's mission in the world.

The missional church movement began in the 1980s when missionary and theologian Lesslie Newbigin observed that Western churches forgot how to be cross-cultural.[8] Returning to England after decades in India, Newbigin observed that churches misunderstood their cultural embeddedness. Once the center of culture, the church expected people to assimilate to congregational customs and beliefs. The church expected people to extract themselves from secular culture and meet the church on its own terms to hear the good news. Empty pews and closing congregations are evidence of the church's misplaced expectation.

Some churches fight off decline. They design worship, special events, ministry programs, and marketing to attract people from the community into their congregation. They thrive at organizational development and marketing, but they still lack a missional mindset. These congregations still expect others to bridge the divide between community and church culture. Unfortunately, these growing congregations often attract people from other struggling congregations. Too often, joining a congregation means being extracted from community relationships and service.[9]

The missional church movement reminds us to engage our surrounding community. We are to animate the good news—to be the good news—for our particular corners of the world. The church's place in society has shifted, and congregational leaders are awakening to the need for changed attitudes and action. This book offers key questions to awaken missional attitudes and action.

---

church as called to be on mission for God in the world.

8. Newbigin, *Foolishness to the Greeks*. See also Newbigin, *The Other Side of 1984*.

9. Missional leaders critique this extractional church model and contrast it to the missional church model. See Hirsch and Ford, *Right Here, Right Now*, 251.

INTRODUCTION

Spirituality

The church's role in spirituality has also shifted. Spirituality has become more individualistic in our society. Engaging our community must also include engaging the hearts of individuals. Spiritual practices no longer need a supportive community or tradition. Spirituality in our secular age is deeply personal, and for many people spirituality can flourish without reference to church or even God.

Spirituality connects people to a deeper purpose and meaning. This purpose, too, can be without reference to God. For example, purpose is found in parenting, community causes, or social issues. Purpose is expressed as a personal mission and vision for the world: healthy children, safe communities, and a just society. Long before the church's mission is on their radar, people are already invested spiritually in their own personal mission and purpose in the world. Congregational mission must connect with this pre-existing spirituality and purpose in parishioners.

A missional church recognizes that God's vision for the world cannot be imposed on others. A congregation's favorite outreach programs should never compete to replace an individual's "already-mission"—the passion or cause driving a person's sacrifice of time, talents and treasures. A missional congregation finds ways to connect with individuals at that spiritual, passionate level, exploring opportunities and partnerships for living out God's vision of a transformed and reconciled world.

Organizational Change

Missional readiness is not a technical problem with a technical solution. Nonetheless, simple organizational changes can help leaders to nurture a missional, adaptive culture. A missional culture helps a congregation to see opportunities for missional partnerships in the community. Culture and human relationships are complex, but this book's missional questions offer a flexible framework around that complexity. Your reflections on the questions asked throughout this book may lead to some technical changes which, in turn, may set the stage for missional adaptation and action.

Addressing these technical issues builds congregational readiness for missional ministry. Most congregations possess the individual skills, resources, and motivation for missional ministry. However, these individual skills and motivations need the support of the organization. Individual parishioners may be able, willing and ready; but does the congregation help or hinder the collective energy needed for missional ministry?

This book is informed by theology and organizational psychology,[10] but the questions do not require a seminary or business school degree. Pastors and lay leaders may use this book's questions as a catalyst for missional development. Congregations may also use a consultant to facilitate the question conversation, goal setting, and subsequent change processes.

Readiness Questions

Each chapter introduces an indicator of missional readiness. A readiness question is linked to each indicator, and questions are posed to clarify and motivate action. This book is not intended as a step-by-step manual for improving congregations. Rather, the readiness questions are designed to spark conversation, goal setting, and preparation for action. This book's value will be in the action it generates.

The book presents five areas of readiness: opportunity, vision, structure, culture, and assets. Each area is related organically. A congregation needs to discern a missional vision and strategy, and that mission strategy needs a supportive ministry structure. Strategy and structure need people and relationships, both within the congregation and out in the community. People and relationships need congregational assets to animate and enact the missional strategy's vision.

---

10. My understanding of readiness and change is influenced by the Transtheoretical Model describing stages of readiness for change. See Prochaska et al., "Transtheoretical Approach," 247–61.

INTRODUCTION

These five areas organize nine readiness questions: already-mission, strategy, focus, ministries, support, people, partnerships, property, and finances. Each chapter discusses desired outcomes, vital behaviors, change and influence strategies, goal setting and related resources.

Each readiness question is structured similarly. Each question includes a set of three possible responses. Responses correspond with red (R), yellow (Y), or green (G)—similar to stop, caution, and go on a traffic light. Individually and communally, you consider the questions and responses that best describe your congregation. The red response suggests a lack of readiness in this area. The yellow response suggests needed innovations will lead to readiness. The green response suggests missional readiness already in this area.

Readiness Question. *This question invites reflection on an area of congregational life, leading to conversations about readiness for mission.*

Lack of readiness, needing improvements.

Minor improvements leading to readiness.

Missional readiness in this area.

Goal Setting. *This question invites conversation about plans or possibilities that exist to improve readiness (or build on strengths in this area).*

Each readiness question includes a follow-up goal setting question. Individual reflections and group conversations will reveal opportunities for action. The readiness questions are designed to

INTRODUCTION

prompt conversation, debate, agreement, and even disagreement. The goal setting questions are designed to prompt action. Readiness questions and goal setting worksheets for use with congregations are included with each chapter and may be photocopied.

Congregations and communities are unique, so this book's missional questions are designed to be broad enough to fit a variety of contexts. The book is aimed at North American, mainline congregations; however, other traditions may find opportunities to revise material for different contexts.

Influencer Questions

Each chapter includes influencer[11] questions. The influencer model provides a powerful tool for mapping change in your congregation. The book's nine readiness questions (Vital Behaviors) focus together on one overall outcome: a congregation with a missional imagination (Desired Outcome). If missional means being God's good news in the community and the world, then missional imagination is the habit of imagining concrete ways that the congregation and its parishioners can be that good news.

Change is produced when people are willing (Motivation) and able (Ability) to perform the vital behaviors that lead to a desired outcome. Change is a process of influencing the motivation and abilities of people at three levels: individual (Personal), relational (Social), and organizational (Structural). These three levels of motivation and ability produce the target vital behavior, which in turn contributes to the desired outcome. A good change facilitator or consultant will help your leadership team or governing board to design an action plan that considers these key change ingredients.

The following influencer questions help congregational leaders to do the right things with the right people. The more specific you can be with your answers to these questions, the more likely you will cultivate self-motivation and skills in your congregation's parishioners.

11. Patterson et al., *Influencer*.

INTRODUCTION

Desired Outcome
A congregation with a missional imagination.
Vital Behavior
The nine missional readiness indicators.

Personal

Ability	What do you need in order to learn and practice the vital behavior? What do others need?
Motivation	What would make the vital behavior intrinsically satisfying to you? To others?

Social

Ability	How can learning about and practicing the vital behavior be supported by your existing relationships? For others?
Motivation	How can your existing social relationships be harnessed to motivate you to learn and practice the vital behavior? For others?

Structural

Ability	Are your attempts at practicing the vital behavior helped or hindered by your congregation's governance structure? Does the organizational structure support your missional imagination? Does it support missional imagination for others?
Motivation	Are there simple but meaningful incentives for you to participle in the vital behavior? Are your success stories celebrated? Are you aware of the negative consequences of not supporting missional imagination?

INTRODUCTION

While each chapter includes more specific influencer questions, I recommend keeping these general questions before you when considering the book's nine readiness questions. The conversations generated by these questions are helpful starting points for congregational leaders, ensuring that your exploration of mission, ministry, and organizational change remains focused on the people God has called to be your congregation.

Already-Missional

Chapter 1 describes the book's approach to missional action. Rather than focusing energy on new, resource-intensive projects that emerge as the final outcome of a complex strategic planning process, this book keeps congregations focused on the missional activity already happening through individual parishioners and their community partnerships. The readiness questions provided here help a congregation to place collective resources and structures around the already-mission of individual parishioners.

This book begins with the assumption that people are already on mission in their world. Whether that personal mission is focused on parenting, community development, or caring for others, our congregations are filled with passionate people already on mission in the world. Church-centered survival thinking leads congregational leaders to overlook this treasury of missional activity. The Already-Missional chapter explores the relationship between these personal missions and congregational mission strategy.

Creating a Conversation

This book is designed for use by congregational leaders and consultants. There is no prescribed process for engaging participants with these questions. Most congregations have leaders with facilitation skills or access to denominational resource people. Your congregation's unique culture and structure will influence how you create missional conversations.

INTRODUCTION

Preparation. Your facilitator may design a process with a congregation's governing body, focus groups, and/or an entire congregation. Each participant is encouraged to read this book prior to group consultation. If that is not feasible for a large group, then the leadership team and governing body are encouraged to read this book. A facilitator may provide an educational presentation to participants based on this book prior to discussing the readiness questions. Ideally, participants will be introduced to missional principles and the readiness questions prior to the actual consultation. The facilitator should ensure that participants are sufficiently ready to consider each readiness question.

Readiness Questions. Each readiness question can be considered individually and as a group. With small groups, allow time for individual reflection on each question before inviting participants to share responses in the small group. With multiple small groups, also allow time for sharing responses in the larger gathering. It is not necessary for everyone to agree on the same response. Differing perspectives will provide a thicker, richer reflection on the question. A skilled facilitator goes a long way to achieving a meaningful and constructive process.

Goal Setting. Your responses to this book's readiness questions are an important part of your congregation's ongoing missional conversation. Each of the book's nine readiness questions includes a goal setting question. Each goal question invites conversations and planning around desired outcomes, action, indicators, responsibility and accountability, timeline, and evaluation.[12] The worksheets that follow each chapter may be photocopied and used as a workbook to capture your thoughts and ideas. Your notes may be collected along with those of other congregational participants to generate discussion and form a consensus on action.

A facilitator can guide conversations about possible action. A small group can be tasked with recording the conversation and proposing formal action. The goal setting worksheets at the back of this book provide a structure for developing goals and outcome measures. Again, an experienced facilitator will add value to the process.

12. For a helpful planning resource, see Coyne and Cox, *Splash & Ripple*.

INTRODUCTION

Follow Up. The question process may be useful semi-annually or annually in your congregation's planning cycle. Responses to readiness questions lead to goal setting and planning, and the goal setting worksheets may be reviewed monthly with the governing body to monitor progress. While conversation is the heart and action is the hands and feet of this process, commitment is the backbone. Commitment includes following up on action plans, and monitoring short- and long-term outcomes. Repeated use of this missional readiness model will provide a basic level of follow up.

Summary

This book is about congregations being God's good news by developing habits that support a missional imagination. The book's nine central questions and dozens of related questions build congregational readiness for missional action. Missional action is directed into the community where the congregation lives.

The book's nine readiness questions promote missional conversations about building upon parishioner already-missions in the community. These conversations are externally-focused and cross-cultural, where congregations step beyond the church's familiar practices and adapt and innovate towards relationships and ministry partnerships with community stakeholders.

If using this book with a facilitator or consultant, congregational leaders can read each chapter individually or collectively. It is possible to use the book with a retreat or over ten meetings to allow missional conversations to ferment. Along the way, participants are encouraged to engage the readiness questions, influencer questions, and worksheets to create concrete action plans built on honest congregational self-assessment.

PART ONE

MISSIONAL OPPORTUNITY

A BOOK CANNOT TELL you what missional action to take. There is no step-by-step manual to prescribe missional ministry. There is no to-do check list. This book is focused on readiness for missional action. Readiness for missional action arises from relationships: relationships within the congregation and relationships beyond the congregation.

Part One is an assessment of your congregation's readiness for ministry in the world. Readiness Question 1 asks about the already-mission of your congregation's people.

CHAPTER 1

Already-Missional

CONGREGATIONS ARE GIFTED WITH mission-minded parishioners who are too often overlooked. These mission-minded folk provide leadership to their community's various social-sector organizations, apart from any connection with or mandate from their congregations. Too often, clergy and parishioners do not connect this community service with congregational mission. Rather than assuming that mission begins only in the church, a missional congregation needs to recognize that God is already on mission in the community. We need an expanded missional imagination to connect congregational life and community service.

Missional vs. Mission Broker

Missional does not mean attracting new members by extracting them from the surrounding community. This attractional-extractional[1] approach promotes ministry strategies and programs aimed at attracting people into a congregation and, consequently, extracting people from their community service. Newcomers who are attracted to the congregation are expected to do the cross-cultural work necessary to adjust to congregational culture. Historically, congregations have relied on the Christian church's cultural

1. Hirsch and Ford, *Right Here, Right Now*.

centrality to exempt congregational leaders from engaging cross-culturally with the community.

The missional critique of the attractional-extractional model includes recognition that a post-Christendom church must equip Christians in congregations to engage cultural diversity in the community. Instead of programs and worship services aimed at extracting potential members from the community and attracting them into congregational life, the missional church emphasizes the need to equip believers to be sent out into the world to proclaim the gospel and co-create the kingdom of God.

Missional leaders do not assume that parishioners are missional blank slates. Missional leaders recognize that parishioners may already be engaged in personal or community activities that parallel congregationally-sponsored ministries or align with the *missio Dei* and God's vision for creation proclaimed by Jesus as the kingdom of God. Missional activity does not begin and end with a congregation. When the extra-congregational community service of the body of Christ is unrecognized, the missional imagination is diminished.[2]

Missional leaders are not mission brokers, connecting blank slate parishioners with congregational ministry opportunities aligned with the congregation's mission strategy. When congregational leaders unilaterally define the mission strategy—and determine what ministry initiatives from within the congregation align with the mission strategy—missional imagination is diminished. Because parishioners' extra-congregational activity remains invisible, the formal congregational vision and mission strategy fall short of accounting for the pre-existing missional activity of all parishioners.

Too often, congregations replicate community services towards offering their own brand or expression of the social service. For example, an elderly outreach program may exist in the

---

2. Bono addressed missional imagination at a national breakfast in Belfast: "And this wise man said: stop. He said, stop asking God to bless what you're doing. Get involved in what God is doing—because it's already blessed." Bono, "Transcript."

community, supported by local government and overseen by local community leaders. Rather than partnering with the existing service, congregational leaders will recruit congregational members to organize a parallel ministry under congregational oversight. Or congregational leaders may organize overseas mission awareness trips for parishioners rather than partner with an existing agency that already has an infrastructure and partnerships aimed at long-term outcomes. The assumption that mission begins congregationally and remains under congregational control seems to drive these replicated rather than partnership mission activities. The message to parishioners already engaged with community agencies is that only congregational ministry is legitimately missional and an expression of faith.

When only the congregational leader's vision and mission strategy are valued, then all congregational resources are expected to align accordingly. Parishioners, although already on mission at home or in the community, are expected to align their time, talents, and treasures with the congregation's formal mission strategy. Congregationally-recognized missional service requires the re-alignment of parishioner assets currently committed to their extra-congregational activity. Parishioners and their available gifts are seen as a means to a congregational end. Consequently, parishioners find their extra-congregational mission activity to be in competition with their congregation's mission strategy. Both are competing for the parishioner's limited time, talents, and treasures.

Already-Missional

The already-mission idea recognizes that parishioners and non-parishioners are often already engaged in self-sacrifice towards a felt-mission. Whether or not a particular activity is an expression of Christian mission, the self-sacrifice towards others represents a personal mission that may reflect God already at work in the world. The focus shifts from boundary metrics ("Is my community service within congregational boundaries?") to growing potential for alignment with and covenanting within the *missio Dei*.³ The already-mission lens shifts the pastoral leadership question from, "Is your mission properly Christian?" to, "How can your personal mission be a starting point for a missional partnership?"⁴

Parishioners in mainline congregations are typically active in community service outside the congregation.⁵ Parishioners in mainline congregations often serve as volunteers and in leadership positions in community not-for profit organizations. While many parishioners may be motivated to service by their faith, most have learned that public expressions of faith are discouraged in an increasingly secular culture. Parishioners find their faith is not always recognized by social sector organizations, and their social sector activity is not always recognized as missional ministry by congregations. Parishioners conclude that their community service does not count as Christian service.

Already-mission thinking recognizes the connection between community service and congregational mission. Most congregational members are already engaged by a personal mission in addition to (and often prior to) their congregational participation. Already-mission thinking understands this community service as evidence that God's Spirit blows where it chooses, unbounded by congregational structures and strategies. Already-mission thinking recognizes that community and family service contributes to realizing the proclaimed kingdom of God.⁶

---

3. See bounded versus center set thinking in Schmelzer, *Not the Religious Type*, 165.

4. The Judeo-Christian story of God's covenant is rooted in the story of Abraham and Sarah. When God called Abram and Sarai to participate in a covenant, the couple was already on a personal mission travelling towards Canaan.

5. An American study found that 79% of surveyed parishioners were involved in community service, social service, or advocacy through groups outside the congregation. Woolever and Bruce, *Field Guide*, 68.

6. See Otto Scharmer, *Leading From the Emerging Future*, 2. Scharmer advocates for a shift in economy from satisfying ego or individual desires to consideration of the interests of larger ecosystems. Already-missional thinking draws a congregation away from its ego focus on maintenance and survival to the larger economy of God's activity in the lives of parishioners beyond

Already-mission thinking understands that mission strategy includes partnering with parishioners who have community partnerships. These partnerships are covenantal. Already-mission thinking recognizes that a congregation as a whole and its parishioners individually are engaged in parallel ministries that realize the kingdom of God. This recognition opens the possibility for partnership, and this partnership opens the possibility over time for mutual participation in a covenantal relationship and mission.

Already-mission thinking extends beyond current parishioners to non-members. Non-members are recognized as potential mission partners. Moreover, newcomers to congregations are recognized as "sent": people on mission in the community are called by God and sent to congregations where they nurture relationships with other called and sent people who, in turn, are nurtured and further equipped to be sent back into the community on mission for God. If sent by God, newcomers and established members—along with their already-mission—are considered essential to a congregation's mission strategy.

Readiness Question

Missional action is not the recreation of tasks and realignment of people's energy. Missional action is already lived out daily by the people called by God and sent to and through our congregations. Our first readiness question measures two indicators related to missional action: community service and missional integration.

---

the congregation. Similarly, the process of partnering with a parishioner's already-mission helps to draw that individual's ministry into a larger economy of interests.

PART ONE—MISSIONAL OPPORTUNITY

Readiness Question 1. *Is your already-mission valued as a contribution to your congregation's mission strategy?*

My church and community passions conflict, so I have to give up one to do the other.

I keep my community and church activity separate.

My community service is valued as congregational ministry.

Goal Setting. *What plans or possibilities exist to connect your already-mission to your congregation's mission strategy?*

Community service. Your already-mission may be lived out in your family, community, or broader world. Whatever and wherever your mission is, it is the giving of time, talents, and treasures to the service of another.

Integration. Is your community service recognized by your congregation? Do you see your already-mission as an expression of your faith? Missional congregations make space for the recognition and nurture of individual missions, integrating these into the congregation's mission strategy.

Discerning Already-Mission

If leaders are to create space for the already-missions of people inside and beyond the congregation, then leaders need vocational discernment skills to help parishioners articulate their already-mission. An entry point into understanding a person's particular already-mission is the question, "What would you die for?" To understand what I will die for is to understand what I value most. Most people never have to die for what they value most. Nonetheless, everyone suffers (perhaps dies slowly) for what they value most. For example, parenting is a most common already-mission among parishioners and newcomers. Parents understand what it means to suffer for the sake of their children—loss of freedom, diminished social life, lack of sleep, financial costs. Most parents will acknowledge that they are willing to die for their children's safety and well-being—evidence that parents value their children.

There are, of course, people prepared to self-sacrifice or even die for personal missions that are offensive to the good news of Jesus Christ. These are not the norm, and a congregational leader can readily discern between these. Nonetheless, even the most challenging tensions between a personal already-mission and a Christian understanding of *missio Dei* must be addressed from the perspective that God has called and sent this person to participate in a local congregation's mission. The question, "What would you die for?" leads through missional listening and pastoral discernment to the question, "How can our congregation partner with you on your already-mission?"

These missional questions apply broadly to discerning God's mission for the church. When we ask Christian scriptures, "What would God die for? What does God suffer for?" we find the covenantal, prophetic, and gospel texts reveal a God who values creation, humanity, and the marginalized through self-giving and self-sacrifice. When we ask how the scriptures imagine the best possible future for a thriving creation, humanity and the marginalized, the scripture texts about redemption and healing reveal a vision of the kingdom of God. When we study the scriptures to understand God's commitment to realizing the envisioned kingdom of God, we find incarnational and passion texts about an incarnated God-with-us who commits self-beyond-assets on mission towards realizing the kingdom of God. Moreover, we find baptismal and commissioning texts that call us as disciples into this mission and its various expressions of ministry. The question, "What would God die for?" leads through missional exegesis to the question, "How can our congregation partner with God's already-mission?"

PART ONE—MISSIONAL OPPORTUNITY

Mission-shaped leadership aims for a congregational mission strategy that builds a bridge between the questions, "How can our congregation partner with God's already-mission?" and "How can our congregation partner with you on your already-mission?" Pastoral leaders listen to hear connections between expressions of the kingdom of God and the parishioners' values and vision. Space is opened to explore mutual support and shared benefits of partnering for mission. The question becomes, "Can our congregation help to sustain you on mission?"

People are gifts from God, not a means to our ends. The already-missions and ministries that people bring to congregational participation are gifts—not competitive threats to a congregation's mission. As gifts, these already-missions and their bearers are understood within God's gift-economy, and we are called to be good stewards of these gifts. Good stewardship includes adding value to these already-missions. To add value, missional-minded leadership brings parishioners and their already-missions into conversation with the gospel, and that encounter is formative. Bringing a parishioner's already-mission into conversation with the gospel has a spill-over effect: there is an accompanying formative influence on the culture and practices of the community in which the already-mission is enacted.

Already-Missional Questions

An already-missional conversation can happen between pastors and parishioners, between parishioners, or with people outside the congregation. By developing public and private relational space in congregations for already-mission conversations, missionally-minded people move naturally to partnering with one another.[7] The already-missional conversation is guided by four questions:

1. What is so important to you that you're willing to sacrifice (time, talents, treasures) significantly for it?

---

7. See Wenger et al., *Cultivating Communities of Practice*, 58 for discussion of private and public relational space.

2. Where do you serve others beyond church-sponsored activities? (For example, parenting, neighborhood, community, workplace, world.)
3. How does this service relate or connect to your faith?
4. How has your congregation sustained you in this service (if at all)?

People refer frequently to children and grandchildren as relationships of sacrifice, and service beyond the-congregation range from helping frail neighbors, volunteering with social service agencies, and charitable contributions to teaching and health-care employment as vocation. Long-time members of a congregation sometimes struggle with the second question, unable to identify service that is not church sponsored.

Clergy sometimes struggle with the second already-missional question, unable to identify personal service that is not church sponsored. Not surprisingly, most leaders in paid, accountable ministry have already located a sense of calling and purpose in and through congregational participation, and they have aligned their lives with congregational ministries. These leaders have a clear sense that their already-sacrifices of time, talent, and treasures—including relationships—have been in response to God's call to ministry. This clear connection for congregational leaders can become an obstacle to understanding Christian service beyond the scope of the church.

People often relate service to faith using common biblical expressions like, "love your neighbor as yourself" and "caring for orphans and widows." Many people identify their congregation as a sustaining support for their work in the world, usually through worship participation or encouragement from a pastor. Still, many describe a disconnect between congregational participation and community service, with some expressing disappointment that their congregation failed to appreciate or know their community service.

Designing for already-mission attitudes and habits takes into consideration multiple factors that influence organizational behavior. A congregational leader can be a catalyst for change by unilaterally engaging multiple parishioners in conversations driven by the mission-minded questions provided above. Eventually, these already-missional conversations shape organizational culture and readiness for growth and maturity.

Influencer Questions

This book's goal is the development of congregations with a missional imagination. Missional-minded parishioners produce missional congregations. Strong and healthy congregations in this post-Christendom culture are able to imagine fresh, new ways of being on mission for God in the community and the larger world. The already-missional conversations described in this chapter offer a helpful habit for nurturing missional imagination.

If missional conversations are an essential ingredient for developing missional imagination, then congregational leaders need to encourage these conversations. The following questions encourage leaders to imagine strategies for influencing parishioners individually and congregations collectively to initiate missional conversations.

Desired Outcome
A congregation with a missional imagination.
Vital Behavior
Having already-missional conversations.
Personal
Ability   Can you as a congregational leader practise already-missional conversations with other leaders in the congregation?

Motivation	What would motivate you to talk with other parishioners about your personal mission and passion? How can conversations about personal ministry and passion add value and support to your already-mission?
Social	
Ability	Can you move beyond practising already-missional conversations with other leaders to initiating and modeling these conversations with other parishioners, especially newcomers? Can you talk about your personal already-mission in a way that builds mutual support?
Motivation	Can you help others to see that conversations about their already-mission can add value and support for their personal ministry passion?
Structural	
Ability	How can the congregation as an organization encourage and support missional conversations? How can it be built into people's calendars or programming? What space in the building is best suited for these conversations, and is that space inviting? Are the congregation's governance and core ministries ready to support the partnerships that may arise from these conversations?
Motivation	Do leaders of the congregation's governance and core ministries appreciate the value of missional conversations? How can organizational structures work together to encourage personal conversations between parishioners about their already-missions? If appropriate, are the variety of parishioner already-missions celebrated publicly?

PART ONE—MISSIONAL OPPORTUNITY

The chapters that follow explore how your congregation's governance and core ministries can become ready to support the initiatives arising from these missional conversations. Missional change making in congregations involves a shift in personal thinking, relational support, and organizational functioning.

Summary

This chapter is about stewardship of parishioner ministry at home, in the community, and in the world. Already-missional thinking assumes that God is already at work in the community, calling parishioners and potential parishioners to serve where they live. Congregational mission begins where God's spirit is already at work.

This chapter's approach to missional conversations begins with conversations about people's already-mission. Congregational leaders look for the kingdom of God breaking through into our world when parishioners give their time, talents, and treasures to be God's good news in the lives of others, whether privately or through work with social sector organizations. Community organizations may not see their work as motivated by faith, but congregations can still find opportunities to partner towards a common good.

Apart from a first session or meeting that provides a general introduction to the readiness questions, influencer questions, and worksheets, participants are encouraged to start with this chapter on already-mission, which is the concept that informs the rest of the book. Facilitators or individual readers may want to refer back to this chapter when exploring the ideas presented in the following chapters.

Goal Setting Worksheet 1

Already-Missional

Readiness Question 1. *Is your already-mission valued as a contribution to your congregation's mission strategy?*

R — My church and community passions conflict, so I have to give up one to do the other.

Y — I keep my community and church activity separate.

G — My community service is valued as congregational ministry.

Goal Setting. *What plans or possibilities exist to connect your already-mission to your congregation's mission strategy?*

Desired Outcome

What is your desired outcome? Be specific.

Action

What action is needed to achieve desired outcome?

Already-Missional

Indicators

> How will you measure short-, medium-, and long-term outcomes?

Other

> What other issues need consideration?

Responsibility and Accountability

> Who takes action?
> To whom are the project leaders accountable?
> What deadlines?

PART TWO

MISSIONAL VISION

GOD HAS AN IMAGINATION. God imagines our world transformed. God's vision for the world is called the realm or kingdom of God. Jesus describes the kingdom of God using many different images: mustard seed, treasure, leaven, net, and within you. No single word or image fully captures this mystery of God's imagination.[1] Congregations are called to participate in the realization of God's imagination in the world.

Part Two is an assessment of your congregation's strategic readiness for missional ministry. Readiness Question 2 asks about your congregation's mission strategy[2] and participation in regu-

---

1. Alan Roxburgh tells the story of a sophisticated, retired corporate CEO who demanded a definition of *missional* during a workshop. Roxburgh asked the group to study a set of biblical parables and come up with a definition of the kingdom of God. When the group could not settle on a definition, Roxburgh told the CEO, "Until you can give me a definition of the kingdom of God, I can't give you a definition of missional." Roxburgh and Boren, *Introducing the Missional Church*, 34–35.

2. Organizational development often gets bogged down in nomenclature debates about vision, mission, purpose, strategy, objectives, goals, outputs, outcomes, etc. Without fueling the debate, I will take vision to be what we imagine as a desired outcome, mission as being sent to achieve the vision, purpose as the sense of meaning and identity that extends from this vision and mission, strategy as formal and informal plans to accomplish the mission, objectives and goals as tactical steps along the way, outputs as planned

PART TWO—MISSIONAL VISION

lar missional conversations. Readiness Question 3 asks if your mission strategy is focused internally on survival or externally beyond the walls of the church.

---

and executed events or programs, and outcomes as the short- and long-term hoped-for and surprise consequences of action.

CHAPTER 2

Missional Strategy

GOD HAS A MISSION. God's mission (*missio Dei*) is to realize what God imagines, the kingdom of God. God's mission also has a church, the body of Christ.[1] The church is God's mission strategy, and we are called to join God on mission. God is a missional God, and the church exists to fulfill God's mission in the world.

How does the church participate in God's mission strategy? The church begins with a missional imagination. A missional church imagines God already at work in the world. A missional church imagines our world transformed as God's world. Then the missional church finds ways to realize this vision: the hungry fed, drink for the thirsty, the naked clothed, strangers welcomed, captives set free, mourners comforted, creation healed. We strategize to become the good news for the world.

Being the church, then, means nurturing this missional imagination for action. Missional congregations are continually envisioning the world transformed. Leaders of missional congregations are continually imagining what the good news looks like

---

1. Moltmann writes, "It is not the church that has a mission of salvation to fulfill in the world; it is the mission of the Son and the Spirit through the Father that includes the church." Moltmann, *Church in the Power of the Spirit*, 64. Similarly, Dearborn writes, "It is not the Church of God that has a mission in the world, but the God of mission who has a Church in the world." Dearborn, *Beyond Duty*, 8.

in their community and world. Missional leaders engage their congregations in missional conversations. As one retired organizational consultant in my congregation says, "Keep the conversation going, and the Spirit will speak."[2]

Visioning for mission can be a big conversation that gathers a congregation with a formal process to create a formal mission strategy. Or missional visioning can be many small, informal conversations that respond to emerging community needs, guided by an informal mission strategy. Some experts argue that strategic planning is wasted energy in a world of discontinuous change. Today's changes are rapid and no longer related incrementally to the status quo. Traditional strategic planning assumes continuous, incremental change over an extended period, allowing us to extrapolate from the present and predict future conditions. Continuous improvement can meet the need for continuous change, but we live in a world of discontinuous change where organizations need skills for continuous innovation.[3] Your congregation's mission strategy is not as important as the missional conversations that keep visioning evergreen. These conversations include prayer and study, storytelling, and reflection. Missional conversations are individual and group discernment of God's call to be good news in the world.

Readiness Question

Missional leadership includes building congregational readiness and capacity for these missional conversations. There is no right or wrong way to lead a congregational conversation about mission strategy. What is important is that the conversation happens and engages the congregation. Our second readiness question

---

2. Credit to Trevor Jordan, parishioner at Grace United Church, Sarnia, Canada for teaching me this saying.

3. Alan Roxburgh argues along similar lines but from a missiological perspective that strategic planning does not support missional action. Roxburgh, *Missional Map-Making*, 73–85.

measures two indicators related to missional conversations: frequency and level of participation.

Readiness Question 2. *When was the last time your whole congregation participated in a visioning or mission strategy conversation?*

More than three years ago.

Two years ago.

One year ago.

Goal Setting. *What plans or possibilities exist to engage your congregation in visioning or mission strategy conversations?*

Frequency. Our world is continuously changing. When the surrounding community undergoes demographic, economic, political, health, and other cultural changes, a congregation needs to revisit and re-envision mission strategy and goals. A lot can change in three years. I recommend that a congregation-wide conversation about mission happen at least every three years. If your congregation or leadership is reading this book and discussing responses to these readiness questions, then you are half-way there.

Level of participation. Different people have different levels of congregational participation.[4] Some people attend weekly

---

4. Wenger describes four groups needing differing invitations to participation: small core group (10-15% of congregation), small active group (10-15% of congregation), large peripheral group (70-80% of congregation), and people outside the community who are partners or "intellectual neighbors". Wenger et al., *Cultivating Communities of Practice*, 56.

and serve in leadership positions. Some attend regularly and pay close attention to leadership decisions and congregational meetings. Some attend infrequently but monitor the activity of leaders and active members. Some people are not church members or adherents, but they watch from the outside community. It is rare for everyone in a congregation to participate in visioning conversations. But the whole congregation can be invited into a process that recognizes the different levels of congregational participation.

Commitment to Action

This readiness question has a related goal setting question: What plans or possibilities exist to engage your congregation in visioning or mission strategy conversations? Your individual and group reflections on this missional strategy readiness question will reveal opportunities for action.

Perhaps your congregation has not considered mission strategy for many years, and you decide to engage a consultant or design a congregational survey. Can a denominational resource person connect you with visioning tools?

Perhaps your congregation is continually exploring mission strategy. Can you build on that strength? How do you evaluate the effectiveness of these continual conversations? Do you measure outcomes?

Perhaps missional conversations happen accidentally or *ad hoc*. Can you establish a standing committee to be responsible for planning missional conversations and follow up? Can the responsibility be added to an existing committee or position?

Perhaps your congregation has frequent conversations about how to be on mission for God, but the level of participation in these conversations is limited to a particular demographic group. Perhaps only the leadership insiders participate. Can you expand the conversation and demonstrate that input is valued? The more people participate, the more people take ownership of leadership decisions and directions.

Influencer Questions

If ongoing missional conversations are an essential ingredient for missional imagination, then congregation-wide missional strategy conversations are an important way to capture the energy generated by these conversations. When people are in the habit of sharing their already-missions and celebrating the already-missions of others, eventually themes and needs emerge. These themes and needs can help to build a broad consensus about how congregational resources can support parishioners in the community. Mission strategy wraps a plan around these ministry needs.

Remember, mission strategy is a means to a higher end: to cultivate a congregation with a missional imagination, which is the habit of imagining concrete ways that the congregation and its parishioners can be God's good news in the community and world. These influencer questions focus leaders on developing skills and motivation needed for ongoing missional conversations.

Desired Outcome
A congregation with a missional imagination.

Vital Behavior
Regular congregation-wide visioning or mission strategy conversations.

Personal	
Ability	*Do leaders know how to organize congregation-wide conversations? Do parishioners know how to participate and what to share in small groups or plenary discussions?*
Motivation	*Can you explain how a group conversation about congregational mission adds value to an individual parishioner's already-mission?*

	Social
Ability	How can you support leaders who organize group conversations? Can you activate the parishioners who are most likely to model positive participation in congregational discussions of mission?
Motivation	Who are the opinion leaders you need to get on-side to make missional conversations desirable for the larger group?
	Structural
Ability	Are missional resources freely available to you and others? Do leaders study these resources together and share opinions? Does the agenda for leadership meetings include missional issues?
Motivation	How are people thanked for their already-missional work in the community? Is the thank you coming from the right person? Are your success stories celebrated? Are you aware of the negative consequences of not supporting missional imagination?

The next chapter discusses how to focus your congregation's missional strategy beyond maintenance and survival. If your mission strategy is to support and celebrate the variety of parishioner already-missions, then strategy needs to include an external focus. A skilled facilitator can help to design successful mission strategy events.

Summary

This chapter is about congregations being on mission for God. Our mission is sparked by imagination, and that imagination needs to be informed by both the biblical good news stories about Jesus

Christ and the stories of parishioners already being God's good news for others. Missional conversations bring this gospel imagination into the community's awareness, allowing intentional plans to emerge for transforming that imagination into reality.

Facilitators and consultants can encourage flexibility with strategic planning, recognizing that there are many planning processes available. Sometimes various parishioners can be dogmatic about their preferred method of strategic planning, and the ensuing debates over the best method can frustrate the energy and motivation of the larger group of participants. The worksheets included with each chapter provide a basic structure for goal planning and should be sufficient to initiate outcome based strategic action.

Goal Setting Worksheet 2

Missional Strategy

Readiness Question 2. *When was the last time your whole congregation participated in a visioning or mission strategy conversation?*

More than three years ago.

Two years ago.

One year ago.

Goal Setting. *What plans or possibilities exist to engage your congregation in visioning or mission strategy conversations?*

Desired Outcome

What is your desired outcome? Be specific.

Action

What action is needed to achieve desired outcome?

Missional Strategy

Indicators

How will you measure short-, medium-, and long-term outcomes?

Other

What other issues need consideration?

Responsibility and Accountability

Who takes action?
To whom are the project leaders accountable?
What deadlines?

CHAPTER 3

Missional Focus

You have probably heard the comparison of the church to a grease factory that only manufactures enough grease to lubricate its own machinery.[1] The comparison is unflattering but too often true. Increasingly, congregations struggle to manufacture enough grease even for internal use. The missional church does more than manufacture surplus grease to share with the community. The missional church works in partnership with other community stakeholders to lubricate healing and transformation—what partners might call social welfare or the common good, and what the church understands as the good news and kingdom of God.

The word mission is easily misunderstood today. The church's use of the word is associated with overseas missionaries proclaiming the gospel of Jesus Christ on behalf of home congregations who provide financial support. Or the word mission is reduced to a description of the outreach programs supported by a congregation. Similarly, mission strategy is reduced to a plan describing which outreach programs a congregation will support. Even then, the mission strategy of many congregations is to wait and see what surplus grease is available to ship into the community or overseas.

---

1. The story's origin is unknown, but a version from a sermon by John E. Harnish is credited to a pastor named Stan Bailey. See Harnish, "Goin' Fishin.'"

MISSIONAL FOCUS

The word missional attempts to differentiate itself from the current understanding of mission. The missional congregation coordinates all of its ministries and resources—not just outreach and social justice programs—for enacting God's mission in the world. Similarly, missional strategy is a plan or narrative describing a way of being God's good news in the community and world.

During the development of this book, many congregational leaders misinterpreted missional strategy questions to mean only outreach ministry. When asked, "Do you have a mission strategy?" they responded, "Yes we do. We have an outreach committee and they plan outreach projects and fundraising." Upon closer examination, the congregation lacked a missional strategy or vision that permeated all dimensions of congregational ministry. Outreach was mere surplus grease to give away after all internal ministries were maintained.

To understand this chapter's readiness question properly, mission strategy cannot be misunderstood as a description of one congregational ministry among others. If the church is God's mission strategy in the world, then everything a congregation is and does is informed by an understanding of God on mission. Not just outreach programs. God's mission shapes worship, education, fellowship, and outreach ministries.

Is the congregational mission strategy or vision that influences all of your congregation's ministries focused internally or externally? In a missional congregation the focus is external, beyond merely lubricating the well-being of insiders. The mission strategy greases the wheels of ministry, but those ministry wheels turn the congregation outward to the community and world.

Readiness Question

A basic indicator of missional readiness is an externally-focused rather than internally-focused mission strategy. Again, this indicator can be misunderstood as referring only to outreach or social justice ministry. Even a strong outreach program can be internally-focused if the ultimate goal of the outreach program is

PART TWO—MISSIONAL VISION

to serve the congregation's reputation in the community or create a value-added experience for church volunteers doing the outreach.

A third missional readiness indicator is a mission strategy that actually informs all ministries. A mission strategy or vision that collects dust and never guides day-to-day activity is wasted. Our third readiness question measures these two indicators related to missional strategy: external focus and influence on governance and ministries.

Readiness Question 3. *Is your congregation's missional strategy focused internally or externally?*

R — *Mission strategy? Most of our energy goes to surviving.*

Y — *We have a mission strategy, but it does not influence all ministry.*

G — *Our missional strategy focuses all our ministry on the community and the world.*

Goal Setting. *What plans or possibilities exist to connect your congregation's ministry activity and committee mandates to an externally-focused missional strategy?*

Focus. The missional congregation is focused on God's activity in the world. When congregations have regular missional conversations, a missional plan or strategy eventually emerges. A mission strategy does not need to be a formal strategic planning document. Some congregations relish comprehensive strategic planning documents with clear targets and outcome measurements. Some congregations simply need a sentence that fits on a t-shirt.[2] More important than the document's density or length is its missional focus.

Influence on ministry. To influence ministry, a mission strategy must influence the people engaged in those ministries. Missional focus and clarity allow people to discern if their ministry activity adds value to the mission plan.[3] Missional focus is not reduced to outreach programs; rather, it enfolds the entire congregation, leadership, and ministries with purpose.

Commitment to Action

This readiness question has a related goal setting question: What plans or possibilities exist for connecting your congregation's ministry activity and committee mandates to an externally-focused missional strategy? Your individual and group reflections on this missional strategy readiness question will reveal opportunities for planning and action.

Perhaps your congregation has a clearly focused missional vision, but your ministries still operate as silos. What conversations need to happen to overcome competing interests and purposes?

Perhaps your congregation is a well-oiled machine with ministries guided by the same strategic plan, but the strategic plan is focused internally. How can you build on this harmony and add a missional focus to your strategic plan?

Perhaps your congregation is already influenced missionally, and parishioners understand when and how their ministry activity contributes to missional outcomes. How can you build on this

---

2. Organizational expert Peter Drucker advises that "The effective mission statement is short and sharply focused. It should fit on a T-shirt. The mission says *why* you do what you do, not the means by which you do it." Drucker et al., *The Five Most Important Questions*, 14.

3. Drucker adds that "The mission is broad, even eternal, yet directs you to do the right things now and into the future so that everyone in the organization can say, 'What I am doing contributes to the goal.' Every board member, volunteer, and staff person should be able to see the mission and say, 'Yes. This is something I want to be remembered for.'" Ibid., 14.

PART TWO—MISSIONAL VISION

success to strengthen relationships internal and external to the congregation?

Influencer Questions

A mission strategy document can say all the right things about focusing energy into the community. But if no one pays attention to that mission strategy, then parishioner energy stays focused on congregational maintenance or survival. An externally-focused mission strategy does not preclude designating resources for internally-focused ministries like pastoral care and faith formation. These internal ministries can still contribute to parishioner readiness for ministry into the community.

These influencer questions explore how the congregation's mission strategy can remain meaningful and influential for parishioners, who are naturally focused on the world beyond the church's walls. The challenge is less how to keep parishioners focused on the community and more how to keep this community focus when parishioners are in the church building making church decisions about church business.

Desired Outcome
A congregation with a missional imagination.
Vital Behavior
Parishioners engaged in ministry under the influence of an externally-focused missional strategy
Personal

Ability	Do parishioners know and understand the mission strategy? Is the mission strategy captured in a brief, memorable sentence?
Motivation	How can the missional strategy connect with your passion for a particular ministry? Connect others?

	Social
Ability	What would help committees to refer regularly to the mission strategy? Do leaders engage in ministry and talk about the mission strategy?
Motivation	How can the process to develop the mission strategy increase your sense of ownership of the mission strategy? Others?
	Structural
Ability	What would help committees to refer regularly to the mission strategy? Do committee terms of reference connect with the broader mission strategy?
Motivation	Does the congregation celebrate parishioner involvement in missional ministry? Do annual reports and budgets acknowledge parishioner ministry beyond internal initiatives? Are you and others warned when "grease" is only being manufactured to lubricate the congregation?

The next chapter will discuss how all of a congregation's ministries can work together to animate an externally-focused mission strategy. The congregation's mission strategy guides and inspires how ministries are structured and resourced. When their already-missions find expression in an externally-focused mission strategy, parishioners look for opportunities to partner their personal time, talents, and treasures with congregational ministry.

Summary

This chapter is about letting community mission influence how congregations do ministry. A congregation's mission strategy cannot be confused with organizational maintenance. An externally-focused mission cannot be reduced to outreach ministries, no matter how successful they are. Congregational maintenance is important, but it cannot be an end in itself. We tend to the health of the congregation and its parishioners so they can be God's good news in the world.

If missional imagination is developed through conversations with the already-mission of parishioners, then the mission strategy will be externally-focused beyond congregational maintenance. An externally-focused mission strategy will resonate with the already-mission of parishioners. An externally-focused mission strategy will help to harmonize the various already-missions of individual parishioners.

Facilitators and consultants can be sensitive to the financial and membership challenges faced by congregations while helping participants keep a focus on the community. The more voices you bring to the strategic planning conversation, the broader the support for the missional strategy. When representatives and opinion leaders from all parts of the organization structure are included in the strategic conversation, the mission strategy is less likely to collect dust on a shelf and more likely to inform the hearts and minds of congregational decision makers.

Goal Setting Worksheet 3

Missional Focus

Readiness Question 3. *Is your congregation's missional strategy focused internally or externally?*

Mission strategy? Most of our energy goes to surviving.

We have a mission strategy, but it does not influence all ministry.

Our missional strategy focuses all our ministry on the community and the world.

Goal Setting. *What plans or possibilities exist to connect your congregation's ministry activity and committee mandates to an externally-focused missional strategy?*

Desired Outcome

What is your desired outcome? Be specific.

Action

What action is needed to achieve desired outcome?

Missional Focus

Indicators

> How will you measure short-, medium-, and long-term outcomes?

Other

> What other issues need consideration?

Responsibility and Accountability

> Who takes action?
> To whom are the project leaders accountable?
> What deadlines?

PART THREE

MISSIONAL STRUCTURE

THE CHURCH IS GOD'S mission strategy in the world. The church's ministries animate and enact that mission strategy. A congregation's organizational structure is built around these ministries. The structure matters, and it influences which ministry initiatives matter enough to receive support. Congregational structure guides our imagination for what is possible. Organizational structure influences congregational culture, which has the potential to be missional.

Part Three is an assessment of your congregation's structural readiness for missional ministry. Readiness Question 4 asks about your congregation's core ministries. Readiness Question 5 asks about the support structure connected to your core ministries.

CHAPTER 4

Missional Ministries

IF MISSION IS WHY we are the church, then ministry is how we are the church. Ministry gives form and expression to mission. Ministry is the embodiment of mission. The church is called the body of Christ. If mission is our purpose, then ministry is the shape or form of that body. The body of Christ needs flesh and bones—form and structure—to animate God's mission in the world.

Bodies come in all shapes and sizes. Congregations are the body of Christ in all shapes and sizes. Despite these differences, congregations share a common, recognizable ministry structure. The ministries common to all expressions of the church are first described in the second chapter of Acts. This story provides the clearest description of the core ministries that shaped the first church and continue into the present.[1]

> So those who welcomed his message were baptized, and that day about three thousand person were added. They devoted themselves to the apostles' teaching and fellowship, to the breaking of bread and the prayers. Awe came upon everyone, because many wonders and signs were being done by the apostles. All who believed were

1. Maria Harris argues that Acts 2 provides "the most detailed description of what the first Christian community did, as a community . . . In the description, Luke gives us the central elements in ministry . . ." Harris, *Portrait of Youth Ministry*, 13.

together and had all things in common; they would sell their possessions and goods and distribute the proceeds to all, as any had need. Day by day, as they spent much time together in the temple, they broke bread at home and ate their food with glad and generous hearts, praising God and having the goodwill of all the people. And day by day the Lord added to their number those who were being saved (Acts 2:41-47).

Five core ministries are described here, and they provide the overall shape of how the church incarnates God's mission in the world.[2] The church identifies these core ministries by five Greek words: *kerygma* ("message," or evangelism, proclamation); *didache* ("teaching," or discipleship, Christian education); *koinonia* ("fellowship," "common," or pastoral care); *leiturgia* ("breaking bread and the prayers," "praising God," or worship); and *diakonia* ("distributing the proceeds to all, as any had need," or service, social justice, outreach).[3]

Mission strategy describes how the local congregation's five core ministries will enact the larger church's common mission and purpose. Because each congregation's community and context is unique, these core ministries are activated differently in each congregation. Before a congregation can articulate an effective mission strategy, missional leaders need to be familiar with the character of these five core ministries.

Five Core Ministries

There is no singular way to enact these five core ministries and animate God's mission in the world. However, this book encourages congregations to nurture all five core ministries. These core

---

2. The appeal to Acts 2 is not to suggest that congregational development is merely an imitation of the early church, with the organizational blue print available in the New Testament. The early church took on various organizational structures, from individual believers to house churches to congregations. Whatever organizational structures developed over time, the church collectively developed these five core ministries to express its mission.

3. Harris, *Fashion Me a People*, 25.

ministries are in the church's DNA. Some congregations express all five of these ministries. Some congregations are more adept at certain ministries. Some congregations lack one or more of these core ministries. This chapter's readiness and goal setting questions encourage the strengthening of all five core ministries.

Leiturgia **ministry.** Missional congregations gather to worship God. Small house churches and large mega-churches alike gather their people together to offer praise to God. At the baptismal font[4] we are identified as God's children. At the communion table we remember Jesus Christ[5] and are reminded of God's presence in our world.

While worship has a personal, experiential dimension, it is more than a private, individual activity. Corporate worship is a public event. In worship we express our relationship to God through praise. We encounter the good news of Jesus Christ, and through prayer, singing, and scripture we catch a glimpse of the kingdom of God, helping us to imagine our mission and God's vision for the world. Worship shapes and forms us for being sent into the world to be on mission for God.

Leiturgia or liturgy means "the work of the people," and it refers to the public participation in the service of worship. The organization of *leiturgia* ministry takes various forms: worship committee, praise team, choirs, music ministry, chancel committee, and sanctuary guild. Leadership for *leiturgia* ministry may involve presiders, preachers, Eucharistic visitors, music directors, lectors, cantors, acolytes, artists, children's worship leaders, wedding and funeral officiants, ushers, and greeters. *Leiturgia* ministry draws on skills for public speaking, prayer, writing, singing, instrumental performance, reflection, art, and movement.

Leiturgia ministry stands at the intersection of the five core ministries. Worship brings together the congregation (*koinonia*)

---

4. Matthew's account of the Great Commissioning includes baptizing. In its simplest form, the baptismal liturgy includes the Trinitarian formula: "in the name of the father and of the Son and of the Holy Spirit" (Matthew 28:19b).

5. Matthew's account of the Great Commissioning includes the call to "remember, I am with you always, to the end of the age," which is expressed in the structure of the Eucharistic prayer as *anamnesis*.

for teaching (*didache*) and proclamation (*kerygma*) to equip us for service (*diakonia*) in the world. *Leiturgia* or worship ministry ritualizes *koinonia, didache, kerygma,* and *diakonia* in sacred time and space.

Worship reminds us that these five core ministries are not merely a means to an end. We do not worship God to achieve a desired outcome. We worship God as an expression of praise and thanksgiving. When the call to worship effects personal and communal transformation, we are sent to apply these gifts to God's mission in the world. Like God's vision of the kingdom of God, already but not yet in this world, worship opens liturgical time and space into our world, our community, and our missional imagination.

Koinonia ministry. Missional congregations provide fellowship and mutual care. People of the early church shared their time, talents, and treasures communally because they shared a common identity and relationship with God. The sacramental communion that is celebrated in worship is lived out as caring community. Being on mission for God requires mutual support for our common mission.

Koinonia means communion or fellowship. Like the gathering at the communion table, the community of faith is a reminder of Jesus Christ: "where two or three are gathered in my name, I am there among them" (Matthew 18:20). A simple definition of pastoral care is the act of reminding another of God's presence.[6] The caring task of reminding one another of God's presence is a shared responsibility.[7]

---

6. See Morrison, "Stewardship Models of Pastoral Care, Counselling and Supervision," 435–46. I argue here that pastoral care is not the restricted domain of clergy or professionals. It belongs to every baptized Christian. Therefore, the definition of pastoral care must be simple enough for an infant to fulfill: I am reminded of God's presence when I look into the face of an infant. This *anamnesis* grounds *koinonia* ministry in the mission call in Matthew's version of the Great Commissioning: "And remember, I am with you always, to the end of the age" (Matthew 28:20b).

7. See Morrison, "The Pastorate as Helping Relationship," 220–34. I argue here that the definition of community is the gathering of gifts and services towards a common good. In congregations, we gather together our time, talents,

The organization of *koinonia* ministry goes by various names: fellowship or membership committee, and pastoral or spiritual care committee. Leadership for *koinonia* ministry may involve pastoral care ministers, Elders, parish nurses, lay pastoral caregivers, and hospital and nursing home visitors. *Koinonia* ministry draws on skills for hospitality, visiting, prayer, facilitating, counselling, activity programming, meal preparation, and being present.

Didache ministry. Missional congregations develop disciples.[8] A disciple is a learner, and *didache* means teaching. *Didache* ministry teaches disciples how to imagine and be God's good news in the world. Education is for mission and ministry. Readiness for missional ministry includes preparing congregations for performing the five core ministries. Discipleship formation is intimately related to congregational development. When the people of a congregation are fashioned for these core ministries, a congregation is equipped to perform God's mission.

The organization of *didache* ministry goes by various names: Christian education committee, spiritual development or formation committee, discipleship program, or small group ministry. Leadership for *didache* ministry may involve Christian education ministers, Sunday school coordinators and teachers, teaching elders, small group leaders, nursery staff, spiritual directors, and camp counsellors. *Didache* ministry draws on skills for understanding faith development, theology and biblical studies, educational philosophy and psychology, modeling Christian practices, curriculum development, and group facilitation.

Diakonia ministry. Missional congregations serve the needs of people in their community and around the world. *Diakonia* means service.[9] The church described in Acts distributed their be-

---

and treasures towards a common mission.

8. Discipleship is at the heart of our shared mission described in Matthew's Gospel: "Go therefore and make disciples of all nations . . . " (Matthew 28:19a).

9. Maria Harris describes *diakonia* ministry as troublemaking. Harris, *Portraits of Youth Ministry*, 173. Advocacy and justice are prophetic, provocative ministries that rattle the status quo. The word *diakonia* means literally to thoroughly kick up dust (by moving so quickly, which is often needed in

longings to anyone in need. This is a prophetic ministry motivated by Jesus' call to "Do to others as you would have them do to you" (Luke 6:31). It expresses the prophetic words in Micah 6:8 "to do justice, and to love kindness, and to walk humbly with your God." *Diakonia* ministry takes seriously the call to feed the hungry, give drink to the thirsty, clothe the naked, visit prisoners and sick, and welcome strangers.

The organization of *diakonia* ministry goes by various names: outreach committee, social justice or action committee, mission committee, soup kitchen, and homeless shelter. Leadership for *diakonia* ministry may involve diaconal ministers, missionaries, overseas personnel, community development workers, parish nurses, and political activists. *Diakonia* ministry draws on skills for physical and mental health care, social work, fundraising, legal support and advocacy, community organizing, social sector management, hospitality, visitation, and being present.

***Kerygma* ministry.** Missional congregations proclaim the good news of Jesus Christ. What is the good news? The good news is Jesus Christ, the word or message of God made flesh. The life and resurrected life of Jesus Christ is good news. The teachings and promises of Jesus Christ are also the good news. *Kerygma* ministry is the proclamation or telling of this multifaceted good news.

Kerygma means to proclaim or announce. The church's *kerygma* ministry is to proclaim the good news of Jesus Christ. Another familiar word is evangelism, which means to tell good news. The church also describes this as testifying or bearing witness[10] to the good news. In an increasingly secular society, where talking publicly about our faith can be alienating, we may feel more comfortable with the idea of being the good news to the world. Even so, *kerygma* ministry includes talking about why we are motivated to feed the hungry and bless the poor.

---

justice ministry).

10. Luke's description of the church's mission includes, "repentance and forgiveness of sins is to be proclaimed . . . " and the disciples "are witnesses of these things" (Luke 24:47, 48). In Luke's further account of the commissioning of the disciples in Acts, Jesus calls the church to be a witness (Acts 2:8).

The organization of *kerygma* ministry is often overseen by an evangelism committee or proclamation ministry. Leadership for *kerygma* ministry may involve clergy, evangelists, preachers, missionaries, and lay leaders. *Kerygma* ministry draws on skills for communicating, testimony or autobiographical storytelling, relationship building, and friendship.

Readiness Question

How does ministry in your congregation compare with the form described in Acts 2:41-47? *Leiturgia* ministry is the gathering of people for worship of God. *Kerygma* ministry is the proclamation of the gospel or evangelism. *Didache* ministry is the teaching and formation of disciples. *Koinonia* ministry is the fellowship and pastoral care of disciples. *Diakonia* ministry is outreach and service to the community. Your congregation probably uses other terms. Our fourth readiness question measures two indicators related to core ministries: comprehensiveness and intentionality.

Readiness Question 4. *Does a workgroup (committee or network) exist to oversee each of these core ministries:* Leiturgia *(worship),* Kergyma *(proclamation, evangelism),* Koinonia *(fellowship, pastoral care),* Diakonia *(social justice, outreach), and* Didache *(Christian education, spiritual formation)?*

None of these ministries is organized or intentional.

Some of these ministries are ad hoc or missing.

All five of these ministries are overseen by committees or a central leadership group.

PART THREE—MISSIONAL STRUCTURE

Goal Setting. *What plans or possibilities exist to establish workgroups or committees related to these core ministries?*

>   **Comprehensiveness.** This readiness question does not prescribe a particular style or method for doing each core ministry. Rather, the focus is simply on whether each core ministry exists. Do all five core ministries operate in your congregation? There is no singular, best way to do ministry. So much depends on your history and community context. The quality of ministry matters, and your commitment to action will likely need to access resources for growing one or more ministries.
>   **Intentionality.** Most congregations have a committee structure, but there are alternatives. Some congregations coordinate all ministry activity through a central decision making body. Some congregations have elders overseeing specific ministries. This readiness factor is about intentionality rather than governance method. The assumption here is that ongoing attention to a ministry happens when leaders are consistently and persistently tending to it (like a standing committee, always responsible and accountable). If a ministry only receives attention or resources intermittently or as difficulties arise (like an *ad hoc* committee), then continuous innovation may be limited. No attention (like no committee) means a ministry probably does not exist or is not resourced by the congregation.

Commitment to Action

This readiness question has a related goal setting question: What plans or possibilities exist to establish workgroups or committees related to these core ministries? Your individual and group reflections on this core ministry readiness question will reveal opportunities for action.

Perhaps your congregation engages all five core ministries consistently and persistently. How do you measure effectiveness from the lens of your mission strategy?

Perhaps your congregation has a central committee that is responsible for all five core ministries. Is attention given to each ministry? Is agenda time designated for each core ministry? Are some core ministries dominating energy and resources at the expense of others?

Perhaps your congregation had a past conflict with leadership in one of these ministry areas. Has the ministry suffered? How can relationships be healed and ministry re-engaged?

Perhaps your congregation expects paid staff to undertake one or more of these ministries on behalf of all members. How might space be opened up for broader participation?

Perhaps your congregation ignores one of the core ministries. Is that accidental or by choice? Are there people in your congregation who are quietly engaged in this ministry who would benefit from access to resources and mutual support?

Influencer Questions

When parishioners are influenced by an externally-focused mission strategy, they look to the congregation's core ministries to animate that external focus. All five of the church's core ministries lend themselves to a mission strategy aimed at being God's good news in the community and larger world. Congregational leaders play in important part in establishing and supporting these core ministries. These influencer questions focus leaders on developing skills and motivation needed for building the core ministries that animate missional imagination.

PART THREE—MISSIONAL STRUCTURE

Desired Outcome		
A congregation with a missional imagination.		
Vital Behavior		
Establish all five core ministries.		
Personal		
	Ability	*Can you identify existing, underdeveloped, and absent core ministries? Can others?*
	Motivation	*Can you appreciate the connection with the early church? Can others?*
Social		
	Ability	*Can a sermon series help the congregation to learn about the characteristics of each core ministry?*
	Motivation	*Can you connect with other congregations who model each of the core ministries?*
Structural		
	Ability	*Does your congregation's constitution, denomination, or history inhibit your practice of a particular core ministry? What needs to change at an organizational level?*
	Motivation	*Can a visual model of the congregation's five core ministries be developed to reinforce growth?*

Simple strategies for keeping congregations mindful of the five core ministries include: organizing weekly announcements using the five key ministry categories (in your congregation's vernacular rather than the Greek); organizing annual reports and narrative budgets using core ministries; and constructing organizational charts that differentiate between core and support ministry committees. Put simply, let these core ministry categories shape how you communicate congregational activity, which sharpens the focus on the mission strategy.

Summary

This chapter is about the church's historic, five core ministries. These core ministries describe how the church puts mission into action. If the church is the body of Christ, then these core ministries describe the general shape of that body in action. When one ministry area is absent or ignored, a congregation's approach to mission may be wanting. Even if you can imagine an important congregational activity beyond these core ministry categories, this book encourages you not to imagine your congregation with fewer than these five.

Facilitators and consultants can remind congregational leaders that there is no singular correct way to do these five core ministries. The history of Christianity and the countless books on these five ministry activities are evidence that more than one method can be successful. Again, various congregational leaders can be dogmatic about their preferred method of ministry, which can frustrate the energy and motivation of the larger group. This book trusts that a congregation will find the best method for a ministry. The primary task is to ensure that each ministry exists, is resourced, and finds its purpose in the larger mission strategy.

Goal Setting Worksheet 4

Core Ministries

Readiness Question 4. *Does a workgroup (committee or network) exist to oversee each of these core ministries:* Leiturgia *(worship),* Kergyma *(proclamation, evangelism),* Koinonia *(fellowship, pastoral care),* Diakonia *(social justice, outreach), and* Didache *(Christian education, spiritual formation)?*

None of these ministries is organized or intentional.

Some of these ministries are ad hoc or missing.

All five of these ministries are overseen by committees or a central leadership group.

Goal Setting. *What plans or possibilities exist to establish workgroups or committees related to these core ministries?*

Desired Outcome

What is your desired outcome? Be specific.

Action

What action is needed to achieve desired outcome?

Core Ministries

Indicators

> How will you measure short-, medium-, and long-term outcomes?

Other

> What other issues need consideration?

Responsibility and Accountability

> Who takes action?
> To whom are the project leaders accountable?
> What deadlines?

CHAPTER 5

Missional Support

If LEITURGIA, KOINONIA, DIDACHE, *diakonia*, and *kerygma* are a congregation's core ministries, then what is everything else? Everything else is either governance or support. Governance is a process that looks at the big picture of congregational mission. Support is a process that manages congregational resources. These governance and support processes provide the ways and means (e.g., permission and funding) for core ministries to function. Governance and support make sure that there is sufficient organizational grease, allowing the core ministries to be on mission productively in the community.

In a missional congregation, governance and support processes serve the needs of core ministries. Not the other way around. The priority of core ministry is a measure of congregational health. As congregations decline in health, energy for vision is slowly replaced with management structures.[1] Children and youth ministry

---

1. See Bullard, "Life Cycle and Stages." Bullard provides a helpful VRPM model for understanding congregational health. New congregations are strongly motivated by an inspiring *Vision*. Strong *Relationships* support this vision, and as membership grows, events and *Programs* develop. To support the growing programs, a *Management* structure develops. Management can become rigid at the expense of vision and relationships. Dying congregations retain management structure long after the people needed for vision, relationships, and programs disappear.

faces this misplaced priority too often. Consider the story of a congregation's summer Vacation Bible School coordinator who returned on day two of the program to find crafts and supplies removed from the church basement by the custodian who steam vacuumed the carpets. Despite the space being booked months in advance for VBS, a culture shaped by misplaced priorities allowed the custodian to prioritize carpets over children's ministry.

Leaders and volunteers who oversee governance and support processes serve an important role. These people want to see core ministries succeed and thrive. Lack of clarity around congregational mission and ministry contributes to these unfortunate conflicts.[2] Efforts to nurture missional conversations and strengthen core ministries yield greater outcomes when priorities are clear.

Readiness Question

Missional congregations understand that governance and support committees exist to fulfill congregational mission—and the core ministries that enact this mission. Healthy congregations practice management habits that serve core ministries and their committees. Support processes serve core ministry committees, and, in turn, ministry committees serve congregational mission. Our fifth readiness question measures two indicators related to missional support: missional integration and level of consultation.

---

2. A typical conflict in conciliar congregational governance models is what I call the "Session vs. Stewards syndrome." In this church model, the Session oversees core ministries, and Stewards oversee property and finances. As congregations mature and decline, management of resources takes priority over core ministries. Instead of Stewards consulting regularly with the Session, the Session is scripted into the role of dependent, having to pursue the Stewards, who play bank or trustee. Because most ministry requires space (property) and funding (finances), the Stewards exercise veto power over ministry initiatives by withholding ways and means. However, projects overseen by Stewards advance without obstacles because resource allocation decisions are internal to that support committee. Over time, energy and leadership for the Session's core ministries atrophy for lack of exercise and innovation.

PART THREE—MISSIONAL STRUCTURE

Readiness Question 5. *Do your governance and support committees have a stake in the mission strategy and consult with your core ministry committees to provide solutions to ministry needs?*

R Governance and support committees work independently from mission strategy and core ministries.

Y Depends on the support committee and core ministry.

G Regularly by all governance and support leaders.

Goal Setting. *What plans or possibilities exist to integrate your governance and support processes into missional ministry?*

Integration. All activity in a congregation is held together by a common vision and mission. If governance and support processes and committees are unaware of or ambivalent towards the mission strategy, they will eventually be at odds with core ministry initiatives.

Consultation. Communication is crucial for mission success. When committees operate as silos, stewardship collapses into competition for resources. Routine and purposeful consultation allows for timely problem solving and meeting ministry needs.

Commitment to Action

This readiness question has a related goal setting question: What plans or possibilities exist for integration of your governance and support committees into missional ministry? Your individual and group reflections on this missional support readiness question will reveal opportunities for action.

Perhaps your congregation's governance structure favors one core ministry over the others. How does this impact the other core ministries?

Perhaps an individual parishioner has invested so much time and money into a particular ministry that congregational leaders are at the mercy of that individual's good will? How can that individual be reminded gently that the congregation's mission strategy cannot take back seat to managing his or her ego or self-esteem?

Perhaps a support committee is not aware of the congregation's mission strategy. How can the support committee's role in the mission strategy be clarified? What is the support committee's *de facto* mission strategy, and how can that be bridged to the larger congregational mission?

Influencer Questions

When the congregation's core ministries are refocused to animate the externally-focused mission strategy, they need the congregation's governance structure to support new ministry initiatives with a wide range of resources. Shared problem solving becomes essential for missional ministry. Silo mentality—the unhealthy habit of pitting various ministry domains against each other for resources—needs to be replaced with shared problem solving and collaboration. Committees responsible for property, finances, staffing, technology, and other support ministries need to be active collaborators with core ministry committees to find solutions to *leiturgia, koinonia, diakonia, didache,* and *kerygma* ministry challenges.

When core and support ministry committees cooperate to produce outcomes that animate the overall mission strategy, the congregation's missional imagination is reinforced and rewarded. These externally-focused ministry outcomes need leaders to imagine more than the maintenance or survival of the building and budget. These influencer questions focus on drawing all stakeholders together into a story larger than the various, independent, and competing ministry silos.

PART THREE—MISSIONAL STRUCTURE

Desired Outcome
A congregation with a missional imagination.

Vital Behavior
Shared problem solving between support committee and core ministry leaders.

Personal

Ability	How can the various core and support ministry committee leaders communicate effectively? How can various committees solve ministry challenges creatively and collaboratively?
Motivation	Do support committee members have a stake in the mission strategy? What makes contact and problem solving a pleasant, constructive experience for you? For others?

Social

Ability	How do you model or facilitate consultative behaviors at governance meetings?
Motivation	How can friendships between core and support ministry committee members be nurtured outside of regular church business?

Structural

Ability	Do support committees have terms of reference and purpose statements that connect their work with the broader mission strategy? Do support committees have representation at the governance table?
Motivation	Do core ministry leaders show appreciation for support? Is the custodian's contribution to the preacher's sermon recognized? How do support committee contributions get evaluated and celebrated in ministry outcome measures?

Before we move to the next chapters on people and partnerships, we need to remember that the above chapters on mission strategy and congregational ministries are also about people and relationships. These influencer questions focus on two important change ingredients with people: the ability to do the vital behavior and the motivation to practise the new behavior. Congregational leaders need to influence ability and motivation with individuals, between people, and in the organizational structure.

Summary

This chapter is about the important ministries that support *leiturgia*, *koinonia*, *diakonia*, *didache*, and *kerygma* ministry. Governance and support ministries serve the mission strategy by resourcing the core ministries. An unclear mission strategy can lead to confusion, placing core ministries and support ministries at cross-purposes. Support ministries, like core ministries, need to see that they have a stake in a purpose greater than any single committee's mandate.

Facilitators and consultants can help congregations to identify when support ministries are disconnected from core ministries. The idea that congregations have core ministries can provoke reactions from people serving on support committees. People serving property, finance, technology, and staffing committees may misunderstand the differentiation between core and support ministries to mean their service is valued less. Similarly, people serving worship, education, social justice, pastoral care, and evangelism committees may misunderstand the differentiation between core and support ministries to mean their roles are more important. In a congregational culture where various core and support ministries operate in silos and compete for resources, the shift to a missional mindset can trigger anxiety. The consultant's role may be most challenging here.

Goal Setting Worksheet 5

Missional Support

Readiness Question 5. *Do your governance and support committees have a stake in the mission strategy and consult with your core ministry committees to provide solutions to ministry needs?*

R — *Governance and support committees work independently from mission strategy and core ministries.*

Y — *Depends on the support committee and core ministry.*

G — *Regularly by all governance and support leaders.*

Goal Setting. *What plans or possibilities exist to integrate your governance and support processes into missional ministry?*

Desired Outcome

What is your desired outcome? Be specific.

Action

What action is needed to achieve desired outcome?

Missional Support

Indicators

> How will you measure short-, medium-, and long-term outcomes?

Other

> What other issues need consideration?

Responsibility and Accountability

> Who takes action?
> To whom are the project leaders accountable?
> What deadlines?

PART FOUR

MISSIONAL CULTURE

GOD'S MISSION STRATEGY HAS people—*is* people. Congregational structure organizes people. Congregational culture shapes people. People and their relationships are complex. No simple definition of God's vision, kingdom of God, the good news, or the word missional exists—because they intersect with the complexity that is people. Ministry is not the simple application of technical solutions to technical problems. Missional ministry requires innovation and adaptive solutions, which take time. People complexity requires experimentation, failure, and learning. Missional congregations need a culture that builds adaptive capacity.[1]

Part Four is an assessment of your congregational culture's readiness for missional ministry. Readiness Question 6 asks about your congregation's adaptability. Readiness Question 7 asks about your people's community relationships and partnerships.

---

1. See Heifetz, "Presentation" for a discussion of adaptive capacity.

CHAPTER 6

Missional People

THIS CHAPTER CANNOT COME close to addressing the complexity of people in congregations. So we will focus on an important human capacity: adaptability.[1] Missional congregations require adaptable people. The culture outside the congregation faces discontinuous change and requires adaptable people. The culture inside the congregation, if it hopes to sustain relationships and partnerships in the community, must be equally adaptable.

Adaptability is the ability to adjust to changing conditions and environments. Adaptability is an important capacity for cross-cultural relationships. The early church, following the call by Christ to go into all the world, excelled at adaptability. Adaptability is related to resilience, which is the capacity to bounce back from stress and hardship. Bouncing back suggests a core that is preserved despite hardship. Missional congregations

---

1. The focus on adaptability is open to criticism. Should not faith be the primary characteristic in a missional congregation? Or *kenosis*, emptying oneself to be open to God's will? Why adaptability, which seems to derive from Darwinian anthropology rather than theological anthropology? Without dismissing these questions, I see adaptability in the sense of fitting or joining: being fitted by, fitting oneself to, being fashioned, joining together. There is something deeply relational and incarnational in adapting. While space does not allow an extended theological reflection, I offer that the choice of adaptability is not without theological consideration.

79

PART FOUR—MISSIONAL CULTURE

nurture the capacity for adapting to change while preserving core beliefs and values.

Adaptability is an important survival skill for an organism, but it is also necessary for an organism to flourish. Missional congregations flourish when their culture and people are able to adapt mission and ministry to the surrounding community. This chapter's readiness question encourages congregational—not merely individual—adaptability for missional ministry.

Congregational change requires new attitudes and habits. New habits will not happen until people are ready.[2] Missional congregations do not rely on compliance to authority, adherence to rules, or power sharing. People in congregations already have power and will adapt when ready. Missional leaders help people to become ready to adapt.[3]

Adaptability relates to identity. Change is easier to navigate when our identity is preserved or continues in some new way. Missional leaders help people to draw connections between their familiar identity and new habits.[4]

Congregational culture shifts when a critical mass of members adapts attitudes, identity, and practices to realize missional goals. Chapter 1 explored how to help this shift by having already-missional conversations with parishioners and newcomers. These conversations help people to connect their personal mission to congregational mission. When this happens, people begin to attach their personal wellbeing to congregational wellbeing.[5]

2. Prochaska et al., "Transtheoretical Approach," 247–61.

3. Ibid. Prochaska argues that these do not work: compliance model (subordinates controlled by professional authority); adherence model (following rules created by experts); empowerment model (leader shares power with followers). They propose a readiness model, where leaders use social influence to help people become ready for change.

4. Ibid.

5. Gervaise Bushe provides a helpful distinction for identification with a group:

> Before a person identifies with a group, the group itself is seen as a potential source of threat and/or opportunity for furthering the person's self-interests . . . A pre-identity group is one in which most

Readiness Question

People in your congregation will have a range of adaptive capacity. Of course, some people in your congregation struggle with change while others are highly adaptive, but how does your congregation function as an organization? Our sixth readiness question measures two indicators related to adaptability: openness to change and preservation of core values.

Readiness Question 6. *How readily does your congregation adapt to changes in the culture?*

See no need to adapt; the world should change.

Open to change but struggle to adapt.

Able to adapt while preserving core values.

Goal Setting. *What plans or possibilities exist to equip your congregation for change?*

---

individuals are not identified with the group and so the aims of individuals are far more salient than the aims of the group in the meaning making taking place. Post-identity groups are those where most individuals identify with the group. By this I mean that they see their personal and social identity as including their membership in this group, and that what effects the group effects them. Here individuals are willing to take the needs of the group into account, sometimes even willing to sacrifice their personal needs, in the ongoing processes of action and meaning-making.

—Bushe, "Meaning Making in Teams," 39–63.

Openness to change. What looks like resistance to change is often resistance to loss.[6] Missional leaders take into consideration people's capacity to absorb change, creating time and space for values and identity questions.

Core values. Missional congregations know what to change for survival and what to preserve for integrity. The church must discern what habits and beliefs need transformation to remain vehicles of God's good news. A changing world requires congregations to be adaptive and flexible without abandoning core beliefs and values. The church must discern what values and beliefs need to be preserved at the heart of the good news.[7]

Commitment to Action

This readiness question has a related goal setting question: What plans or possibilities exist to equip your congregation for change? Your individual and group reflections on this missional change readiness question will reveal opportunities for action.

Perhaps your congregation has a history of adaptation to change. How can this already-capacity be recalled and related to emerging changes in your community?

Perhaps your congregation has a history of running out or burning out leaders who called for change. How can you tend to people's readiness for change prior to asserting the need for change? How can changes be narrated in continuity with your congregation's founding vision or core values and beliefs?

Perhaps your congregation has pockets of people open to change. How can these people be nurtured without creating factions or divisions within the congregation?

Perhaps your congregation has parishioners who are addicted to change for change's sake. How can mature change agents be lifted up in the congregation, highlighting their stories of being

---

6. Heifetz, "Presentation."

7. See Tickle, *Great Emergence*. See also, Tickle, *Emergence Christianity*. Phyllis Tickle argues that the Great Emergence marks our current struggle to reconstruct new answers to theological questions.

good news for someone in the community rather than focusing on the mere idea of change?

Influencer Questions

When a congregation renews or strengthens its relationship with the community, new patterns of thinking, acting, and relating are required. Parishioners are called to adapt to a set of ministry needs larger than the congregation's maintenance or survival. Adaptability is a skill built on new attitudes and habits. These attitudes and habits need to be learned.

These influencer questions explore how adaptive skills and attitudes create an internal congregational culture necessary for an externally-focused mission strategy. Parishioners need an adaptive congregational culture that can respond to and nurture their missional imagination.

Desired Outcome
A congregation with a missional imagination.
Vital Behavior
Adaptive attitudes and responses to changes in the culture.
Personal

Ability	*What resources are available for learning about congregations in a changing culture?*
Motivation	*When have you felt a sense of accomplishment or pride with a past congregational change? What did you appreciate about the experience?*

PART FOUR—MISSIONAL CULTURE

Social	
Ability	Can various generations within the congregation discuss changing culture and shared values? Can people from the community be invited into this conversation?
Motivation	How can parishioners reflect on successful adaptation in their other, non-church organizations? How can this adaptability be imported to your congregation?

Structural	
Ability	How does your congregation monitor community trends and needs? Where do change initiatives get bogged down or vetoed in your formal and informal decision process? Can you generate a case study?
Motivation	What values and beliefs does your congregation need to preserve when adapting to culture shifts? How can the decision process respond to people who habitually take offence to change initiatives? Or people who habitually push change for change's sake?

The above chapters on mission strategy and organizational structure along with the following chapters on finances and property all focus on ingredients needed for an adaptive congregational culture. Strategy, structure, and resources are tools available to people, and a missional culture sharpens these tools to cultivate the congregation's imagination for mission in the community and world.

Summary

This chapter is about adaptability as a people skill. When congregations follow their parishioners' already-missions into the community, they encounter the community's various cultures. Adaptability is the skill that bridges congregational culture into community culture. Congregations can no longer assume they share a culture with the community, expecting the community to accommodate congregational expectations. Congregations and community partnerships are a cross-cultural relationship.

Facilitators and consultants can help congregations to identify the core values that need to be preserved and the secondary values and habits that need to be adaptive. When new, adaptive practices can find clear lines of continuity with past, core values, then change is more readily seen as growth.

Goal Setting Worksheet 6

Missional People

Readiness Question 6. *How readily does your congregation adapt to changes in the culture?*

See no need to adapt; the world should change.

Open to change but struggle to adapt.

Able to adapt while preserving core values.

Goal Setting. *What plans or possibilities exist to equip your congregation for change?*

Desired Outcome

What is your desired outcome? Be specific.

Action

What action is needed to achieve desired outcome?

Missional People

Indicators

> How will you measure short-, medium-, and long-term outcomes?

Other

> What other issues need consideration?

Responsibility and Accountability

> Who takes action?
> To whom are the project leaders accountable?
> What deadlines?

CHAPTER 7

Missional Partnerships

REPUTATION IS LIKE TRUST: earned over time and lost in a moment. A congregation's reputation in a community is a measure of its efforts to be the good news of Jesus Christ. A solid community reputation can be lost in those moments when churches take discriminatory, self-righteous, and uneducated public stands.

Just as damaging, however, is when a congregation's community reputation is lost slowly, over decades, for lack of community relationship. Having no reputation can be just as debilitating as having a negative reputation. When a congregation is forgotten by the community, it may be because the community was forgotten by the congregation. Reputation is relationship, and relationship is reputation.

Partnerships are a form of congregational relationship. Missional congregations form partnerships with organizations to bring the good news to the community and the world. These partnerships may be formal or informal, involving staff, volunteers, and shared resources. They may be long- or short-term, perhaps arising on an *ad hoc* basis. Chapter 1 explored community partnerships formed through parishioners.

The church's theological understanding of partnerships begins with the biblical stories of covenant. The stories of Noah, Abraham and Sarah, Moses, and Israel describe a God who establishes covenants or sacred partnerships. The Christian understanding of covenant is grounded in the good news of Jesus Christ, where God meets us in our world. Covenants or sacred partnerships are central to God's mission strategy. Partnerships need to be central to congregational mission strategy.

Readiness Question

Before a congregation can be ready for missional ministry, it must be ready for relationships with the community. Our seventh readiness question measures two indicators related to community reputation: partnerships and impact.

Readiness Question 7. *What is your congregation's reputation in the community?*

Except for members, closing our congregation would have minimal community impact.

We used to impact the community, and we want to engage the community again.

We are a vital partner in the community's wellbeing.

Goal Setting. *What plans or possibilities exist to explore and create community partnerships?*

Partnerships. Partnership assets[1] include relationships with community groups and leaders, national and international orga-

---

1. Asset mapping encourages community members to recognize their associational and institutional relationships as assets (in addition to physical, individual, and economic assets). Our associations and institutional relationships create opportunities for partnerships between organizations. See Snow,

nizations, denominational ministries and resources, and other institutions and people outside the congregation. Because partnerships are ultimately between people, it is important to remember that our partners are not a means to an end (that is, our goals and desired outcomes). Partnerships are relationships that are mutually beneficial and are nurtured over time.

Impact. As mutually beneficial relationships, partnerships lead to a positive impact in the community. Congregation can be an active partner in community wellbeing. Reputation matters, and a community will assign a positive reputation to a congregation seen as contributing to community wellbeing. The impact is also reciprocal. Change processes within a congregation can be driven by partnership development. Theologically, impact is understood as feeding the hungry, clothing the naked, and caring for the sick (Matthew 25:34-40; Luke 6:20-22).

Commitment to Action

This readiness question has a related goal setting question: What plans or possibilities exist to explore and create community partnerships? Your individual and group reflections on this missional partnership readiness question will reveal opportunities for action.

Perhaps your congregation has a variety of thriving partnerships in the community. How can stories about being the good news for others be told and retold within and without the congregation?

Perhaps your congregation's partnerships are limited to those preferred by key leaders? Perhaps informal partnerships exist through others in the congregation. How might the associational and institutional relationships of everyone in the congregation be valued and considered? How can everyone in the congregation recognize their community within the scope of congregational mission partnerships?

Asset Mapping. See also McKnight, "Asset Mapping," 59–76.

Influencer Questions

Congregational partnerships depend on the relationships formed by parishioners with the community. Parishioners take a personal risk when they invite their congregation into their relationship with a community group or organization. Congregations need to be good stewards of this relationship trust, being careful to add value to an existing partnership.

Community partnerships can be as simple as an individual parishioner's relationship with a community organization. The strength of a congregation's partnership with a community organization is only as strong as the relationships between people. A congregation's reputation in the community is developed through these personal relationships more than media coverage and marketing. These influencer questions focus on the personal relationships parishioners have with community groups. A congregation's missional imagination needs to take root at the intersection of these parishioner and community relationships.

Desired Outcome	
A congregation with a missional imagination.	
Vital Behavior	
Forming and sustaining community partnerships.	
Personal	
Ability	What community partnerships have you already formed and sustained outside of your church involvement? How did you do that? How have others?
Motivation	How have your personal community partnerships added value to your life? To your personal mission? How have others found value and meaning in their community work?

PART FOUR—MISSIONAL CULTURE

Social	
Ability	Where are the opportunities for synergizing your personal community partnerships with those of other parishioners?
Motivation	How can you support and encourage new and existing community partnerships by fellow parishioners? How can they support yours?

Structural	
Ability	Does your congregation pursue relationships with community partners? Are these partnerships nurtured alongside support for your existing, personal community partnerships? Or are they seen as competing?
Motivation	Are individual and congregational community partnerships celebrated? How is the congregation's reputation measured within these community partnerships?

These influencer questions build on the discussion in Chapter 1 about missional conversations and parishioner ministry in the community. These conversations help to reveal the hidden economy of parishioner ministry that congregation's too often overlook. Chapter 9's discussion of financial stewardship will explore this hidden economy of ministry, expanding our understanding of congregational assets.

Summary

This chapter is about congregations partnering with the community through their parishioners. While a partnership may be a formal, structured relationship between the congregation and a community organization, this book is more concerned with nurturing the individual parishioner as the point of partnership. The parishioner is the partnership; the partnership need not be a formal document. A congregation can only manage a limited number of formal partnerships established at an organizational level. Already-missional thinking imagines every parishioner as a partnership into the community. Caring for a parishioner includes caring for the partnership.

Facilitators and consultants can help congregations to widen the scope of community partnerships. If more influential parishioners have organized congregational resources to support their particular community cause, they may need help letting go of their missional monopoly. Sometimes the missional monopoly can extend for decades after the actual partnership or ministry activity has ceased to function. The people who hold title to that now-defunct monopoly can feel threatened by new initiatives.

Goal Setting Worksheet 7

Missional Partnerships

Readiness Question 7. *What is your congregation's reputation in the community?*

Except for members, closing our congregation would have minimal community impact.

We used to impact the community, and we want to engage the community again.

We are a vital partner in the community's wellbeing.

Goal Setting. *What plans or possibilities exist to explore and create community partnerships?*

Desired Outcome

What is your desired outcome? Be specific.

Action

What action is needed to achieve desired outcome?

Missional Partnerships

Indicators

> How will you measure short-, medium-, and long-term outcomes?

Other

> What other issues need consideration?

Responsibility and Accountability

> Who takes action?
> To whom are the project leaders accountable?
> What deadlines?

PART FIVE

MISSIONAL ASSETS

THE CHURCH NEEDS RESOURCES. Being a missional congregation does not mean divesting a congregation of all assets.[1] Missional congregations steward their assets for God's mission in the world. Missional discernment always precedes and determines asset allocation, investment, or divestment. Ideologically-driven divestment, like asset hoarding, can be an obstacle to making missional conversations a priority.

The church may be the body of Christ, but the people who share that body of Christ need places to gather. That takes money and property. How much money and property is a different question, and your congregation's assets may range from no budget or building (e.g., house church or pub church) to a mega-church teaming with staff, revenue, and campuses. Whatever your context, this section is concerned with how finances and property assets are leveraged for missional ministry.

Part Five is an assessment of your congregation's resource readiness for missional ministry. Readiness Question 8 asks about your congregation's financial stewardship. Readiness Question 9 asks about your congregation's stewardship of property.

1. Some church movements like Simple Church, Organic Church, and house church de-emphasize buildings and even see buildings as impediments to healthy Christian communities. See Viola, *Reimagining Church*.

CHAPTER 8

Missional Property

PEOPLE SOMETIMES CONFUSE PROPERTY survival with congregational survival. People form strong attachments to property, which means that the complexities related to human relationships apply to property. Humans are creatures of space, and attachment to God (another way to describe experiencing God's presence) can be anchored in congregational space. Attachments are powerful human processes, and change initiatives involving property need to account for the human condition. A leader's insensitivity to human attachments can threaten safety and provoke anxious reactivity to a change initiative. These strong, human attachments to place and space, however, can also be a source for missional energy. Congregational property is often a key ingredient in community partnerships, and property can contribute significantly to community wellbeing initiatives. Changes to property can open missional thinking.

The missional property readiness question relates to the chapter on missional support. Property is often central to animating each of the five core ministries. Sanctuaries, store fronts, and people's homes gather people for worship. Christian education wings, pubs, and camp grounds gather people for learning the faith. Soup kitchens, homeless shelters, and residences allow outreach ministries to meet human needs. Fellowship halls,

PART FIVE—MISSIONAL ASSETS

lobbies, and youth group rooms gather people for mutual care and support. Church architecture, green space, and church signs announce God's presence and good news to the community. These property resources support the five core ministries, which animate congregational mission strategy.

Readiness Question

Property assets include building space, building conditions, parking, physical plant, grounds, housing, sanctuary, camp grounds, and so much more. Property assets are not a means unto themselves. Rather, they are valuable insofar as they resource mission and ministry. Our eighth readiness question measures two indicators related to missional property: missional integration and stewardship.

Readiness Question 8. *How does your congregational property relate to your congregational mission?*

Our property competes with our ministry and mission.

Our property is an untapped resource for ministry and mission.

Our property serves our ministries and mission.

Goal Setting. *What plans or possibilities exist to connect your property to your congregation's mission strategy?*

Integration. As mentioned in the chapter on missional support, congregational activity needs a common vision and mission. If the purpose of property is at odds with the purpose of core ministries, then missional activity becomes a source for congregational conflict instead of health. Property is often a key ingredient in missional partnerships.

Stewardship. Stewardship begins with what we believe about property, not with how we use or maintain it. The church understands all assets as gifts from God, entrusted to our care for animating the kingdom of God in our world. Our use and maintenance of property extend from this understanding: we return these gifts to God and use them for God's purposes. Stewardship is intimately connected with missional discernment.

Commitment to Action

This readiness question has a related goal setting question: What plans or possibilities exist to connect your property with your congregation's mission strategy? Your individual and group reflections on this missional property readiness question will reveal opportunities for action.

Perhaps your congregation's property benefits one core ministry more than the others. How does this impact the other core ministries?

Perhaps your property committee sees the building as something needing protection from the wear and tear of ministry. How can committees and groups be reminded of the building's purpose and relationship to the mission strategy?

Perhaps your congregation's property is dedicated to the memory of past members. Perhaps various furnishings were purchased by individuals who seem to hold authority over their use. How can these members or the stewards of their memory be engaged in missional conversations to explore the repurposing of this property to connect past and present mission?

Influencer Questions

Congregational partnerships often involve space sharing. Whether building space is shared at no cost with community groups for one-time events or rented long-term to community organizations, the mission strategy needs to guide space sharing. Congregations are used to managing building space for internal ministries or for rental to outside groups for revenue generation. However, the stewardship of space for missional partnerships requires new priorities and building policies beyond congregational maintenance or survival.

The following influencer questions keep in mind that congregational property is about people, and people are called to be on mission for God. Stewardship of property is a Christian practice that responds to God's call on the missional imagination of parishioners and the congregation.

Desired Outcome	
A congregation with a missional imagination.	
Vital Behavior	
Stewarding congregational property for missional strategy.	
Personal	
Ability	*What do you need to learn about congregational property and usage? What do others need to learn?*
Motivation	*How does your congregational property brings you joy? How does it bring joy to others, inside and outside the congregation?*

	Social
Ability	Who are the "historians" of your congregational property, who can tell the story of how property was acquired in response to the congregation's founding mission strategy?
Motivation	How is your spirituality supported or hindered by congregational property? How does it support or hinder others' spirituality?
	Structural
Ability	How are property stewardship criteria linked to the broader missional strategy? How are property committee leaders linked with core ministry leaders?
Motivation	How can the decision process respond to people who habitually claim privileged oversight of congregational property use? Or people who habitually push to divest for ideological or morally imperative reasons?

These influencer questions echo the discussion of ministry support committees in Chapter 4. The committee that manages your congregational property needs to keep the mission strategy in view when making decisions about the building. Property committees need to help core ministries to find solutions to *leiturgia, koinonia, diakonia, didache,* and *kerygma* ministry challenges.

Summary

This chapter is about property—and people. The emotional attachment people have with property is powerful. When congregations renew their mission in the community, property becomes an important asset for community partnerships. Communities need gathering spaces that are not commercialized or politicized, where the common good can take priority. Space sharing is a strategy that congregations can use immediately to build their reputation as a valuable community partner. Chances are that your congregational space is already used extensively by the community.

Facilitators and consultants can help congregations to celebrate the many ways their property is already serving the community. Congregations are not starting from scratch with this missional readiness factor, so there may be energy, consensus, and success to build on when planning partnerships. Building wear and tear costs money, but a positive community reputation does not come free.

Goal Setting Worksheet 8

Missional Property

Readiness Question 8. *How does your congregational property relate to your congregational mission?*

R — Our property competes with our ministry and mission.

Y — Our property is an untapped resource for ministry and mission.

G — Our property serves our ministries and mission.

Goal Setting. *What plans or possibilities exist to connect your property to your congregation's mission strategy?*

Desired Outcome

What is your desired outcome? Be specific.

Action

What action is needed to achieve desired outcome?

Missional Property

Indicators

> How will you measure short-, medium-, and long-term outcomes?

Other

> What other issues need consideration?

Responsibility and Accountability

> Who takes action?
> To whom are the project leaders accountable?
> What deadlines?

CHAPTER 9

Missional Finances

ECONOMISTS TRACK ECONOMIC ACTIVITY within a country (gross domestic product or GDP) plus economic activity of citizens abroad (gross national product or GNP). The church tends to obsess over congregational GDP but ignore congregational GNP.[1] We track internal financial data but ignore the missional impact of member's financial activity beyond the congregation's operating budget. What parishioners put in the collection plate gets counted. What parishioners give independently to a charity or cause is not counted.

But what if that independent financial gift to the food bank or hospital campaign is motivated by faith? What do we teach parishioners about the meaning of church or congregation if this activity does not count as congregational mission? Are we only the church when we step inside the church building or contribute to the church's internal operating budget or outreach fundraising?

Of course, there is no practical way to account for all charitable activity by parishioners—nor would people appreciate the invasion of privacy. The impossibility is further compounded when you try to

---

1. GDP estimates the annual value of goods and services within a country's borders. GNP estimates the annual value of the GDP plus net income of citizens abroad. The analogy is not perfect for my purposes: I'm not concerned with parishioner income or revenue flowing into the church's budget. Rather, I want to draw attention to a missional reality and economy beyond the congregation's operating budget.

MISSIONAL FINANCES

imagine calculating the value of all parishioner volunteer time in the community or parenting activity. But the shift in thinking can help parishioners to know that their activity beyond the confines of the church building and budget counts in the congregation's missional economy. The missional economy is imagined from the perspective of the kingdom of God, not the congregational balance sheet.[2]

We like to boast that people need not check their brains at the door when coming to worship. But our parochial view of mission teaches people to check their already-mission at the door when entering the church building. We teach people to think narrowly in terms of congregational budgets rather than God's larger gift economy.[3] When a parishioner gives money to the local hospice or volunteers on the board of the non-profit counselling center, are they merely being good citizens or are they responding in faith to Jesus' call to love others? Accounting for Gross Congregational Mission (GCM) encourages an alternative economic engine in the missional congregation.

Every organization has an economic engine.[4] The economic engine is that core product that leads customers to open their wallets. To increase revenue, organizations identify that key product or service that correlates with the majority of revenue. Because the offering is gathered during Sunday worship, most congregations

---

2. The missional economy is also understood more broadly than congregational programs and worship. To use Fresh Expressions language, they are a mixed economy. See Archbishop's Council, *Mission-Shaped Church*.

3. The reduction of mission to the congregational economy is revealed in the mistaken use of the term "abundance" when undertaking financial campaigns. Abundance is reduced to the idea that people are withholding money from the church budget: "The good news is we have the money, the bad news is it is still in your pockets." For an excellent discussion of superabundance and God's gift economy, see Ricoeur, "Golden Rule," 293–302.

4. Jim Collins encourages for-profit organizations to identify one economic denominator ("profit per x") that, when done well, has the most significant impact on the corporate economic engine. Congregations tend to see the worship service as the economic denominator. Collins argues that non-profit organizations need to connect their resource engine to organizational passion and ability, which I relate to the many and varied already-missions of parishioners. Collins, "Hedgehog Concept," 17–23.

109

believe that the worship service is the congregation's economic engine. This belief assumes that a better worship service equals more income. Therefore, congregational resource allocation favors the worship service, and greater attendance and revenue is seen, mistakenly, as our return on investment.

Missional congregations, however, understand their economic engine from the perspective of GCM. People are motivated to contribute financially to a congregation when they identify that congregation as a partner in their deepest passions and mission in the world. When we count parishioner already-mission and ministry in the community, we help to connect congregational identity with personal passion.

Readiness Question

Financial assets include revenues, spending patterns, identifiable givers, and levels of giving. Financial assets—and the congregation's economic engine—are stewarded within the larger scope of God's gift economy and parishioners' already-mission and ministry. Our ninth readiness question measures two indicators related to missional finances: missional integration and motivation.

Readiness Question 9. *What drives your congregational giving to your annual budget?*

R — *Worried appeals to meet expenses.*

Y — *The quality of our worship service.*

G — *People's personal connection to the congregation's mission objectives.*

Goal Setting. *What plans or possibilities exist to connect your financial support to your congregation's mission strategy?*

Integration. Financial stewardship has a purpose: to support the congregation's common purpose expressed in the mission strategy. As with property, finances are often connected with core ministries. When finances compete with mission and ministry, then conflict or stagnation are inevitable. Our financial stewardship extends from the understanding that money is a gift from God, and we return this gift to God for God's mission. Stewardship is intimately connected with congregational missional discernment.

Motivation. If money is a gift from God, what motivates us to share it? And how do we decide where to share it? People are motivated to give when they see a connection between congregational mission and their personal mission and values. People give to organizations that support their personal mission. Motivation for giving is connected intimately with personal mission discernment.

Commitment to Action

This readiness question has a related goal setting question: What plans or possibilities exist for connecting your financial support with your congregation's mission strategy? Your individual and group reflections on this missional finances readiness question will reveal opportunities for action.

Perhaps your congregation has sufficient revenue for mission and ministry. Do you understand the complexity of your congregation's economic engine? Can you express that complexity in simple terms that lead to a connection between personal, already-mission and congregational mission strategy?

Perhaps your congregation has yet to connect their personal, community service to their faith. How can you include the value of parishioner already-mission in your discussion of financial stewardship and mission strategy?

Perhaps your annual reports focus only on operating and capital expenses. Can you add a narrative budget that describes how your operating and capital expenses impact your parishioners' and congregation's ability to serve the community?

Influencer Questions

People put their money where their passion lives. When parishioners see their congregation adding value to their personal mission and passion, they take a vested interest in the congregation's financial health. Formal and informal congregational partnerships often have financial costs. The stewardship of congregational money is inseparable from the stewardship of relationships. Knowing your people includes understanding their already-missions in the world.

The following influencer questions keep in mind that financial stewardship is about people. Stewardship of congregational finances is a Christian practice that responds to God's call on the missional imagination of parishioners and congregation.

Desired Outcome
A congregation with a missional imagination.

Vital Behavior
Financial giving to support missional strategy.

Personal	
Ability	What do you need to learn about congregational finances and assets? What do others need to learn?
Motivation	What motivates you to give financial support to the congregation? Is your giving motivated by services received? Is your giving related to the missional strategy? What motivates others?

MISSIONAL FINANCES

Social	
Ability	Who are the "historians" of your congregational finances, who can tell the story of how financial priorities were established in response to the congregation's founding mission strategy?
Motivation	How is your spirituality supported or hindered by congregational finances? How does it support or hinder others' spirituality?
Structural	
Ability	How are financial stewardship criteria linked to the broader missional strategy? How are finance committee leaders linked with core ministry leaders?
Motivation	Is the congregation's financial engine designed around the Sunday worship service? How are financial stewardship initiatives linked to missional strategy?

Similar to the discussion of property in Chapter 7, these influencer questions focus on the attitudes and habits of a ministry support committee. The committee that manages your congregational finances needs to keep the mission strategy in view when making decisions about revenue. Finance and stewardship committees need to help core ministries to find solutions to *leiturgia*, *koinonia*, *diakonia*, *didache*, and *kerygma* ministry challenges.

Summary

This chapter is about finances—and people. Church budgets are not the same as church finances. Already-missional thinking recognizes that parishioners are acting on behalf of the body of Christ when they share their money with community organizations, loved ones,

PART FIVE—MISSIONAL ASSETS

and strangers who need financial support to advance the common good—or pay for health care, housing, education, and groceries. Parishioners need to know that this larger picture counts as Christian service. Stewardship and celebration of each parishioner's already-missional activity is a powerful economic engine.

Facilitators and consultants can help congregations to connect church budgets with parishioner stories of ministry in the community and larger world. Talking about personal finances may be taboo, but if given the right conditions people will talk about the already-mission they fund with time, talents, and treasure. Missional conversations are shared testimonies of serving God by serving others.

Goal Setting Worksheet 9

Missional Finances

Readiness Question 9. *What drives your congregational giving to your annual budget?*

R — Worried appeals to meet expenses.

Y — The quality of our worship service.

G — People's personal connection to the congregation's mission objectives.

Goal Setting. *What plans or possibilities exist to connect your financial support to your congregation's mission strategy?*

Desired Outcome

What is your desired outcome? Be specific.

Action

What action is needed to achieve desired outcome?

Missional Finances

Indicators

> How will you measure short-, medium-, and long-term outcomes?

Other

> What other issues need consideration?

Responsibility and Accountability

> Who takes action?
> To whom are the project leaders accountable?
> What deadlines?

Conclusion

READING THIS BOOK WILL not connect your congregation with the community. You need to talk with people in your congregation about this book's readiness questions. Multiple conversations about our already-missions at home, work, and in the community will spark a missional imagination. That missional imagination can lead to creative partnerships with your community.

The book is only a tool, and it needs people to work. The book is designed for pastors, lay leaders, and consultants working in and with congregations to spark missional ministry. Each chapter's missional readiness question and influencer questions encourage group conversation and action planning. The worksheets help you to capture your conversations with yourself and others about being on mission for God in the community.

This book offers to fix a problem that holds back congregations from community involvement. Rather than extracting parishioners from their passions and service in the community to align with a congregational mission strategy, this book values each parishioner's already-missional activity as a foundation for Christian ministry partnerships in the community.

Missional ministry is produced by connecting congregational mission strategy and parishioners' personal mission passions. Chapter 1 introduced the question: Is your already-mission valued

CONCLUSION

as a contribution to your congregation's mission strategy? Missional strategy brings focus and intentionality to missional action. Chapter 2 introduced the question: When was the last time your whole congregation participated in a visioning or mission strategy conversation? A missional strategy that looks beyond the congregation's internal needs is more likely to connect with parishioner already-mission. Chapter 3 introduced the question: Is your congregation's missional strategy focused internally or externally?

The church's historic five core ministries bring organizational structure to missional strategy. Chapter 4 introduced *leiturgia, kerygma, koinonia, diakonia,* and *didache* ministries with the question: Does a workgroup (committee or network) exist to oversee each of these core ministries? These core ministries need resources to support their missional outcomes. Chapter 5 introduced the question: Do your governance and support committees have a stake in the mission strategy and consult with your core ministry committees to provide solutions to ministry needs?

The people who undertake these various congregational ministries need the influence of a missional culture. Chapter 6 introduced the question: How readily does your congregation adapt to changes in the culture? When congregations adapt to the community culture, without abandoning core values, partnership opportunities arise in response to the congregation's changing reputation. Chapter 7 introduced the question: What is your congregation's reputation in the community?

A final section on missional assets discussed the role of congregational property and finances in mission and ministry. Chapter 8 introduced the question: How does your congregational property relate to your congregational mission? Chapter 9 introduced the question: What drives your congregational giving to your annual budget?

These nine readiness questions are the beginning of a long-overdue conversation in our community congregations. Let me end this book by repeating the wisdom of the retired organizational consultant in my congregation: "Keep the conversation going, and the Spirit will speak."

Bibliography

Archbishop's Council. *Mission-Shaped Church: Church Planting and Fresh Expressions in a Changing Context*. New York: Seabury, 2009.

Bono. "Transcript: Bono remarks at the National Prayer Breakfast Remarks." Transcript of remarks to National Prayer Breakfast. USA Today, February 2006. http://usatoday30.usatoday.com/news/washington/2006-02-02-bono-transcript_x.htm.

Bullard, George. "The Life Cycle and Stages of Congregational Development," 2001. http://sedefca.org/wp-content/uploads/2008/08/stages_of_church_life_bullard.pdf.

Bushe, Gervaise R. "Meaning Making in Teams: Appreciative Inquiry with Pre-Identity and Post-Identity Groups." In *Appreciative Inquiry and Organizational Transformation: Reports from the Field*, edited by Ronald Fry et al., 39–63. Westport, CT: Quorum, 2001.

Collins, Jim. "Issue Four: The Hedgehog Concept–Rethinking the Economic Engine Without a Profit Motive." In *Good to Great and the Social Sectors: A Monograph to Accompany Good to Great*, 17–23. New York: HarperCollins, 2005.

Coyne, Kathy and Philip Cox. *Splash & Ripple: Using Outcomes to Design and Guide Community Work*. Plan:Net Limited, n.d. http://www.smartfund.ca/docs/smart_outcomes_guide.pdf.

Dearborn, Tim A. *Beyond Duty: A Passion for Christ, a Heart for Mission*. Mission Advanced Research and Communication Center. Monrovia, CA: World Vision, 1998.

Drucker, Peter F., et al. *The Five Most Important Questions You Will Ever Ask About Your Organization*. San Francisco: Jossey-Bass, 2008.

Guder, Darrell L., ed. *Missional Church: A Vision for the Sending of the Church in North America*. Grand Rapids: Eerdmans, 1998.

BIBLIOGRAPHY

Harnish, John E. "Goin' Fishin.'" Unpublished sermon, April 7, 2013. http://www.fumcbirmingham.org/wp-content/uploads/2013/01/Goin-Fishin.pdf.

Harris, Maria. *Fashion Me a People: Curriculum in the Church.* Louisville: Westminster John Knox, 1989.

―――. *Portrait of Youth Ministry.* New York: Paulist, 1981.

Heifetz, Ron. "Professor Ron Heifetz Presentation." MadstonBlack, n.d. http://www.madstonblack.com/professor-ron-heifetz-presentation.html.

Hirsch, Alan and Lance Ford. *Right Here, Right Now: Everyday Mission for Everyday People.* Grand Rapids: Baker, 2011.

McKnight, John. "Asset Mapping in Communities." In *Health Assets in a Global Context: Theory, Methods, Action,* edited by Anthony Morgan et al., 59–76. New York: Springer, 2010.

Moltmann, Jurgen. *The Church in the Power of the Spirit: A Contribution to Messianic Ecclesiology.* London: SCM, 1977.

Morrison, Bradley T. "The Pastorate as Helping Relationship." In *The Helping Relationship.* Edited by Augustine. Meier and Martin Rovers, 220–34. Ottawa: University of Ottawa Press, 2010.

―――. "Stewardship Models of Pastoral Care, Counselling and Supervision: The Commonians Meet Ricoeur at Worship." *Pastoral Psychology,* 53 (2005) 435–46.

Newbigin, Lesslie. *Foolishness to the Greeks: The Gospel and Western Culture.* Grand Rapids: Eerdmans, 1986.

―――. *The Other Side of 1984: Questions for the Churches.* Geneva: World Council of Churches, 1983.

Patterson, Kerry, et al. *Influencer: The Power to Change Anything.* New York: McGraw-Hill, 2008.

Persichetti, Laura. "Diverse Faiths Share Gathering of Hope for Haiti Event." *Sarnia Observer.* January 30, 2010. http://www.theobserver.ca.

Prochaska, Janice M. et al. "A Transtheoretical Approach to Changing Organizations." *Administration and Policy in Mental Health and Mental Health Services Research,* 28 (March 2001), 247–61.

Rayjon ShareCare. "Gathering of Hope for Haiti." Rayjon ShareCare Archives, 2010. http://rayjon.org/2010/12.

Ricoeur, Paul. "Ethical and Theological Considerations on the Golden Rule." In *Figuring the Sacred: Religion, Narrative, and Imagination,* 293–302. Translated by David Pellauer. Edited by Mark I. Wallace. Minneapolis: Fortress, 1995.

Roxburgh, Alan. "Why Strategic Planning Doesn't Work in this New Space and Doesn't Fit God's Purposes." In *Missional Map-Making: Skills for Leading in Times of Transition,* 73–85. San Francisco: Jossey-Bass, 2010.

Roxburgh, Alan and M. Scott Boren. *Introducing the Missional Church: What It Is, Why It Matters, How to Become One.* Grand Rapids: Baker, 2009.

BIBLIOGRAPHY

Sandborn Deborah. "Top 50: Jorge de Guzman (Canada's Champions of Change)." *Canadian Broadcasting Corporation.* November, 2010. http://www.cbc.ca/change/2010/10/jorge-de-guzman.html.

Scharmer, Otto and Katrin Kaufer. *Leading from the Emerging Future: From Ego-System to Eco-System Economics.* San Francisco: Berrett-Koehler. 2013.

Schmelzer, David. *Not the Religious Type: Confessions of a Turncoat Atheist.* Carol Stream, IL: SaltRiver, 2008.

Snow, Luther K. *The Power of Asset Mapping: How Your Congregation Can Act on Its Gifts.* Herndon, VA: The Alban Institute, 2004.

Tickle, Phyllis. *Emergence Christianity: What It Is, Where It is Going, and Why It Matters.* Grand Rapids: Baker, 2012.

———. *The Great Emergence: How Christianity Is Changing and Why.* Grand Rapids: Baker Books, 2008.

Viola, Frank. *Reimagining Church: Pursuing the Dream of Organic Christianity.* Colorado Springs, CA: David C. Cook, 2014.

Wenger, Etienne, et al. *Cultivating Communities of Practice: A Guide to Managing Knowledge.* Boston: Harvard Business School Press, 2002.

Woolever, Cynthia, and Deborah Bruce. "Figure 6.4: Serving the Community" In *A Field Guide to U.S. Congregations: Who's Going Where and Why.* 2nd Edition, 68. Louisville: Westminster John Knox, 2010.

Wright, Heather. "Organizers Hope the Movie *Bully* Sparks Discussion." *Sarnia This Week,* 2010. http://www.sarniathisweek.com.